VOLUME 1

2ND EDITION

IMAGES OF FAITH

Reflections Inspired by Lilias Trotter

Miriam Huffman Rockness

PUBLISHED BY

ISBN 978 1 7344001 5 1

Library of Congress Control Number: 2020903291

All Scripture quotations, unless otherwise indicated, are taken from The Holy Bible, New International Version®, NIV®. Copyright © 1973, 1978, 1984 by Biblica, Inc.™ Used by permission of Zondervan. All rights reserved worldwide. www.zondervan.com

Scripture quotations marked (KJV) are taken from the King James Version.

Second edition published by Lilias Trotter Legacy, Inc. ©2020
First edition published by Oxvision Books ©2017

Find us at: **liliastrotter.com**

DEDICATED TO

Brian & Sally Oxley whose vision and generosity have made it possible to reintroduce the life and art of Lilias Trotter to a new generation.

CONTENTS

Foreword	v
Introduction	ix
Prelude: Our Works Will Follow Us	1
Images of Joy	9
Beholdings!	11
Sunshine of My Happy Heart	19
The Speech of Angels	25
February Flowers	33
Bound and Yet Unbound	41
The Gladness of My Joy	49
Glad in the Present Day	55
Images of God	63
The Dew of the Spirit	65
Our God Sees	71
Safe Am I	77
Seeking Shepherd	85
Spring of Life	91
Lesson of the Crab	97
The Price of Power	105
Images of Redemption	113
Harbinger of Spring	115
Glimmer of Light	123
God's Workmanship	131
The Myrrh of Heartbrokenness	139

Beauty from Brokenness	147
Stored Energy	153
The Pain of Parting	161
Images of Spiritual Growth	169
August Oranges	171
Growing Points	179
How Silently, So Silently	187
The Roots of Spiritual Creation	195
Soul Food	201
Expect God to Triumph	209

FOREWORD

IMAGES OF FAITH: Reflections Inspired by Lilias Trotter is the rare volume that illustrates some of the significant ways that spiritual truth may impact our daily realities. Indeed, all of these reflections are taken from the ordinary moments of life—and because of this, they are easily accessible to us.

    Miriam H. Rockness, who serves as guide to these offerings, has been reading and pondering the words of the Anglican artist and missionary Lilias Trotter for three decades. In *Images of Faith*, we reap the benefit of Miriam's dedicated investment of time as we, too, are invited to consider the deep meaning of Lilias's life, and not just the biographical facts.

    In *Letters to Malcolm*, C. S. Lewis's most comprehensive statement on the Christian discipline of prayer, he writes: "We may ignore, but we can nowhere evade, the presence of God. The world is crowded with Him. He walks everywhere *incognito*. And the *incognito* is not always hard to penetrate. The real labour is to remember, to attend. In fact, to come awake. Still more, to remain awake."

FOREWORD

Lilias Trotter understood this truth well, and she spent a lifetime using her artistic gifts to reveal the presence of God that she found everywhere … gloriously made known in the beauty of creation as well as in the lives of the people around her. In *Images of Faith,* Miriam Rockness invites us to learn this art of seeing, so that we are able, as C. S. Lewis declared, "to attend … to come awake … still more, to remain awake" to the reality of God's presence in our own lives. This is an invitation well worth accepting.

MARJORIE LAMP MEAD
INTERIM DIRECTOR
THE MARION E. WADE CENTER
WHEATON COLLEGE, ILLINOIS

INTRODUCTION

IMAGES OF FAITH: Reflections Inspired by Lilias Trotter is an inside view of Lilias Trotter's personal pilgrimage, culled from her diaries, journals, and published works, written and painted over the forty years of her life in Algeria. It is also my pilgrimage of faith as I reflect on those writings and watercolors.

I first became acquainted with Lilias Trotter through out-of-print books, by and about her, in the late 1980s. I was a busy pastor's wife and mother of three children. What could a single woman (no children) from a wealthy West End London family, who lived among the poor of Algeria more than one hundred years ago, possibly say to me? What did an artist whose raw talent captured the attention of John Ruskin have to say to me, struggling to capture a little beauty in my corner of the world?

As it turned out, a great deal! Her insights based on eternal verities of Scripture and tempered with hard-won life experience cut through current trends of thought to the very essence of my soul. It had the ring of truth, and I simply couldn't get enough of her practical perspective.

INTRODUCTION

She wrote of discouragement, struggle, perseverance, joy, love, prayer, the paradoxes of size and significance, of power and weakness—from God's point of view—and, well, just about every topic that mattered to me. She illuminated many of these eloquently worded truths with exquisite watercolors. Lessons from God's Word and God's world—an inward and outward vision—became clear through parables from nature.

    She became a mentor to me, fleshing out truth in the arena of day-to-day living. I wanted to know more about her and find everything written or painted by her. I wanted to share my discovery with others. Thus began a quest that led eventually to my writing her biography and compiling some of her writings and watercolors—a journey that is documented, in part, in the film of her life, *Many Beautiful Things* (2015).

    Fast forward several years. Our children are grown and raising families of their own in three different states; my husband is retired; we have moved to a small town in central Florida. Once again I turn to Lilias, as I process challenges (and joys) of transition and adjustment in this new chapter of my life. I determined to indulge myself in writing reflections on the writings and watercolors that have special resonance for me now—and in seasons past. And, once again, I find that Lily's lessons still hold.

The duty of a biographer is to present an objective account of the subject's life—to paint a realistic portrait—faithful to the facts. I now have the luxury of approaching the themes and topics of her life from a purely subjective point of view: what they mean to me on my journey—present and past. My selection of these topics is purely personal: words and art that have spoken deeply to me and guided me on my pilgrimage of faith.

Lilias wrote two comprehensive treatises on the Christian life: *Parables of the Cross* (an English devotional) and *The Sevenfold Secret* (for the Arab Sufi mystics). She considered these two books to be her most important works, with a definitive purpose and focus.

Images of Faith, in contrast, is an inside view of her spiritual formation, her process of integrating scriptural precepts with life experience. It is a close-up and personal glimpse of Lilias

INTRODUCTION

Trotter's pilgrimage of faith: an adult lifetime of daily learning until the very end of her time on earth. It is also my pilgrimage: how she has guided me through almost three decades of life. My selections were initially determined not by set topics or chronology but by my own journey and how she spoke to my spirit. These selections fell roughly into eight major topics: joy, God, redemption, spiritual growth, prayer, service, refreshment, and faith. In this volume I present four of these topics, the others to follow, as volume 2, within the year. While these categories don't comprise a comprehensive statement of her spirituality, they are representative of the themes that guided her life.

So I share my reflections because I believe they hold universal truths relevant to all pilgrims, regardless of where they are on the journey. I invite the reader to examine with me the "images of faith" culled from her legacy—written and visual.

 # PRELUDE: OUR WORKS WILL FOLLOW US

...for their deeds will follow them.
REVELATION 14:13

*Our works will follow us. God may use, by reason of the wonderful
solidarity of His Church, the things that He has wrought in us, for the blessing of souls
unknown to us: as these twigs and leaves of bygone years,
whose individuality is forgotten, pass on vitality still to the new-born wood-sorrel.
God only knows the endless possibilities that lie
folded in each one of us!*

PARABLES OF THE CROSS

AT FIRST GLANCE, THE PAINTING on the previous page appears to be but dead twigs and leaves. Then one notes a sap green sprig of *"new-born wood sorrel"* above which are printed words from the book of Revelation: "Their works do follow them." Lilias concludes her book *Parables of the Cross* with words that were both prescient for her and potentially for all who follow Christ: *"The results need not end with our earthly days. Should Jesus tarry our works will follow us ..."*

Even as Lilias developed these thoughts, inspired by both God's Word and works, she was no doubt integrating the same with her own life experience: difficult conditions, little apparent results. Her intended break, the summer of 1895, extended into the autumn then winter months including "bed rest"—doctor's orders. Weakness and sleeplessness reflected the strains of ministry yet permitted the prolonged period of rest during which she penned her devotional classic.

The belief, based on Scripture, that what one sows for eternity continues beyond one's earthly span motivated and sustained her as she scattered seeds over the face of Algeria for decades. She saw lives touched by the *"light and life and love"* of God and ministries developed that furthered and deepened that vision. When she died in 1928, thirty members of the Algiers Mission Band continued to minister through fifteen stations and outposts along the coast of North Africa and down into the Southlands, later merging with what is now Arab World Ministries. There are reports in present-day Algeria of God's Spirit working throughout the land, even indications of a fledgling church. She left a written legacy of English devotional books, most notably the *Parables of the Cross* and *Parables of the Christ-life* plus her consummate masterpiece for the Sufi mystics, *The Sevenfold Secret*.

I have no reason to believe that as she recorded the daily events of her life in the small page-a-day leather-bound diaries, she would have imagined that her personal legacy—her life defined in words and watercolors—would be revived a century later. Yet this is what is happening even as I write. God is using *"twigs and leaves of bygone years"* for His purposes: *"the blessing of souls unknown to us."*

Things have been happening quietly and unobserved over the past three or four decades converging into a story of how, through the *"wonderful solidarity of His Church,"* God continues to use her life and legacy. More than thirty years ago, a devoted English missionary remained in Algeria, at the onset of political turmoil, to close down the work and pack up the archives (including Lilias's diaries and journals) to ship out to safety, ultimately in England. Not long after that, on another continent, two American sisters passed on their library of Trotter books to a (then) young minister's wife and mother of three children. Her passion for these books and hunger to learn more about their author and subjects led her, eventually, to the archives in England and to the publishing of a biography of Lilias Trotter, *A Passion for the Impossible,* plus *A Blossom in the Desert*, a compilation of her writings and paintings long-hidden in relative obscurity in three cardboard boxes!

Fast forward to 2014. Brian and Sally Oxley "discover" Lilias through these books and envision a film short to introduce her to the people of Japan, believing her art will appeal to their artistic sensibility, and their hearts. This led to our meeting—a union that sparked other exciting discoveries, journals and sketchbooks, the "missing" Ruskin letters to Lilias—eventually expanding the original concept into an hour-long documentary, *Many Beautiful Things,* which premiered internationally and in the USA at the Manchester and Heartland film festivals, respectively, summer and fall of 2015 and was launched nationwide at the National Gallery of Art, February 2016.

Many Beautiful Things presents the people and land of Lilias's beloved North Africa through her exquisite art, using techniques and equipment unimagined during her lifetime. It is the story of this remarkable woman who made a life-altering decision about the role of art in her life—and how God used both her art and her life for purposes being realized even now after all these years. But above all, it is the story of *God* and how He continues to work His purposes still unknown to us in His time and His way. Only God knows the endless possibilities that lie in her life and legacy.

And(!) "*God only knows the endless possibilities that lie folded in each of us!*" We have no idea how God will use those things we do and say, great or small, for His purposes. We do know that what is sown for eternal purposes will "*pass on vitality*" after our own "*individuality is forgotten.*" And that is what counts: to be faithful to our understanding of His plan for us.

I conclude with Lilias's final challenge in the *Parables of the Cross:* "Shall we not let Him have His way? Shall we not go all lengths with Him in His plans for us—not, as these 'green things upon the

PRELUDE

earth' in their unconsciousness but with the glory of free choice? Shall we not translate the story of their little lives into our own?"

God only knows the endless possibilities that lie folded in each of us!

Lord, thank You for the spiritual legacy of Lilias Trotter. Help me to discover the possibilities You have enfolded within me.

IMAGES OF Joy

# BEHOLDINGS!

For since the creation of the world God's invisible qualities—his eternal power and divine nature—have been clearly seen, being understood from what has been made, so that men are without excuse.

ROMANS 1:20

... going day by day for what the Japanese would call "beholdings" & bring(ing) back vivid word-pictures of the same that are a joy ... They went with the intent of shewing Margaret [sister] a row of wonderful cypresses, silhouetted against the curve of the bay, with the port lying below, the tracery of breakwaters & shipping basins shewing prune coloured on the opal sea.

DIARY EXCERPTS FROM OCTOBER 1925

BEHOLDINGS! LILIAS, IN THE CITED diary entry, was content to enjoy word-pictures of "beholdings" that her sister brought from her excursions to her bedside, she being too weak to venture beyond the four walls of her room. And, from the window of that same room, Lilias observed "beholdings" that gladdened her heart: *Lovelier than ever, this year, has seemed the interweaving of autumn & spring, till you can hardly tell which it is—the tiny stars of white jonquils into the withered grass—& the golden crocus among the falling leaves, & the amethyst Judas blossom, not knowing what to do with itself, from the wealth of sap that the first rains have brought rising."*

Lilias brought to her final years a practice of a lifetime or, in the words of Flannery O'Connor, "a habit of being." From her earliest years, she recorded what she saw in little pocket sketchbooks, capturing a host of "beholdings"—a skill that John Ruskin noted in his "The Art of England" lecture to be "what we should all like to be able to do …" All the while she was training her eyes to see: a "habit" that brought joy even to her most difficult days.

I write at my kitchen table. A photograph, a handful of shells, and a heartful of memories—beholdings!—are what remain of a family vacation, twenty-one people strong, at a Florida beach house. I try to capture images in my journal, sounds and sights: waves pounding the shore; sea birds swooping down for their evening catch; sea grapes flanking the boardwalk leading to the beach; laughter (and wails) of children; these same children nut-brown from the sun, seated around a large wooden table, appetites teased from fresh air and salt water; adults gathered, after the children are bedded, talking late into the night.

What I do by intent—collect beholdings to record and remember—our young grandchildren do by instinct, still awed by everyday wonders. From the porch rocking chair overlooking the beach, I was eyewitness of wonder and firsthand recipient of children's beholdings. They came to me—a convenient anchor—to proffer their treasures: sea glass, an odd configuration of moss, a crab shield, shells of all shapes and sizes. Breathless with excitement, they announced the miracle of hatching sea turtles making their tenuous maiden voyage out to sea.

What occurs on a vacation or scenic trip can be, *should* be, cultivated on a daily basis. Call it "grace" or "blessings" or "gifts"—or, as did Lilias, "beholdings"—it is less about the name than the reality. Beauty is within our reach regardless of our immediate circumstance. It exists in the simplicity of ordinary rites and routines. I believe that beauty is one of God's loveliest ways of reminding us that He is … and that He cares … Pointers, in a sense, to heaven. And, in turn, I'm convinced, that being attuned to beauty is no small thing—whether in the grandeur of a mountain range or the minutia of a cobweb, the nuzzle of a beloved pet or, in the words of Sara Teasdale, "children's faces looking up holding wonder like a cup …"

Sometimes beauty surprises us. Serendipity. Sometimes it seduces us, as did the glimpses of joy that C. S. Lewis, as a child, saw in Beatrix Potter's illustration of Autumn, intimating to him "something other." Beauty sustains us during times of unrelenting duress: the renewal of spring during a seemingly endless war, evidenced by green shoots and yellow daffodils breaking through cracks in barricades of sandbags—described by V. Sackville-West in her *Country Notes in Wartime*. And sometimes it *saves* us: Viktor Frankl's glimpse of "the mountains of Salzburg with their summits glowing in the sunset, through the little barred windows of a prison carriage …"; fragments from a Beethoven concerto, piercing the darkness of a concentration camp barrack, heard by Elie Wiesel; a pot of tulips in a hospital room …

Whether by surprise or design, I am continually startled by "beholdings." If I could, I would paint them, like Lilias, but instead I record them in my journal. "Beholding" I write in bold print; then I jot it down, one at a time, as it happens: scent of orange blossoms …

a single orchid bloom, survivor of a neglected plant … a trio of butterflies dancing above lantana … a peacock reclining alongside a back country road … a clean child wrapped in terry cloth, wet hair slicked behind ears … a letter in the mailbox … recorded music filling the house … a cat sunning in a patch of sunlight …

St. Augustine said: "The soul is weighed in the balance by what delights her. Delight or enjoyment sets the soul in her ordered place." Little matter if we translate that delight in paint or print, in music or in spoken word. What matters is that we do behold. And *wonder*!

God, the world is full of Your glory! May the beholdings I witness today point me to You, the Creator.

SUNSHINE OF MY HAPPY HEART

The heavens declare the glory of God;
the skies proclaim the work of his hands.

PSALM 19:1

The peaks of the Mischabel were just shouting for joy this morning in radiant snow, after a day's storm, and the late filaments of cloud were dancing round their crests. Oh it is a wonderful world.

DIARY AUGUST 28, 1901

TRAVEL JOURNAL 1896, 1897

AUTUMN CHASED US SOUTHWARD, TINTING leaves with traces of color—just as we were leaving. Illinois … Indiana … Ohio … West Virginia … Indian summer it was for us Floridians, just missing the long-awaited cool of a new season.

Until today. Autumn has finally caught up with us—in Florida! Temperatures fell during the night, and this morning I walked out to a cool fall day. A flash of color caught my eye. I reached down and lifted autumn into my hand: a single leaf aflame with crimson tinged in gold. A cardinal, bright as the leaf, darted above my path: autumn on the wing!

Oh, it *is* a wonderful world! Whether the snowcapped mountain Lilias recorded in words and watercolors or the color-washed Florida leaf resting in my hand—all stands still in one's heart brimming with the beauty. I want to freeze the moment—the autumn-ness of it—capture it in a photo or painting or poem. But I know that my best efforts would fall short of the reality. Such moments can't be captured as much as simply remembered. Remembered for the jolt of joy, the momentary transcendence from common cares and exertions that mark one's ordinary days.

Capture an elusive heart-catching moment? No. But cultivate? Yes. Cultivating an awareness of all that is best, is what we not only were created but instructed to do. The apostle Paul echoed the psalmist in urging an awareness of "whatever is true, whatever is noble, whatever is right, whatever is pure, whatever is lovely, whatever is admirable—" adding, "if anything is excellent or praiseworthy—think about such things" (Philippians 4:8).

Consider the pages of my well-worn red leather journals. So quick am I to take to pen to hack out my problems, to process my pain. So stingy with my joy, the pull of gravity favoring the negative. Yet both exist, side by side.

I must learn to live fully my joy in the moment. And train myself to record the positive beholdings of the heart alongside the beholdings of my eye. It is a choice, really, a matter of focus as there is much, indeed, to weigh down one's spirit. But there is so much to elevate one's soul as well. John Ruskin once observed about a gutter: "If you look deep enough, you may see the serious blue of far-off sky and the passing pure clouds. It is at your will what you see in that despised stream, either the refuse of the street or the image of the sky."

"It is at our will," what we choose to see, upon what we choose to focus. Easy, one might say, for Lilias to exult in the dancing clouds and radiant snow of Switzerland. But she brought the same eyes to a North African landscape that many considered parched, dull, even hostile. Her lifelong friend, Constance Padwick, noted: "For her, God's world in every aspect was supremely worth the watching. His ways in nature were her poetry. His ways with humankind were her romance." At the end of her life, Lilias marveled, "Oh how good it is that I have been sent here to such beauty!"

It is at my "will" what I choose to consume me. I can be bogged down with the weight of unfinished work … hurting or hurtful people … worries or concerns about the future … Or I can be elevated by the wonders of this world—the leaf on the ground, the bird on the wing … the unmerited love of grandchildren … friendships nourished by e-mail or phone, a meal or a visit … a loving God revealed through outward vision and inward quickenings …

Pain and suffering will always be present in this broken world. At least for now. But so will the beauty and the wonder. Which do I choose to see when I gaze into the pooled water: "the refuse of the street or the image of the sky"? Which do *you* choose?

Sunshine of my happy heart. God, of my praise, to Thee be praise. —Amy Carmichael

# THE SPEECH OF ANGELS

*I will sing and make music to the L*ORD.

PSALM 27:6

We are lodged in rooms off the Central Hall [at Miechovitz in northern Germany]—& before it is daylight the chorales begin there softly like birds singing in the dawn ... and all day long there is a ripple of gladness.

DIARY NOVEMBER 14, 1908

PAINTING FROM THE VOICE OF THE BIRD AMONG THE FLOWERS

LILIAS ENDED AN INTENSIVE TWO-MONTH speaking schedule in Scandinavia, in the autumn of 1908, with an unexpected trip to Germany. Encouraged by Baroness Kurcks of Sweden, Lilias consented to a meeting with Sister Eva of Friedenshort. This was the beginning of a lifelong friendship and the continuing source of inspiration for both of these remarkable women with similar affluent backgrounds.

Miechovitz was in a mining district on the spur of the Carpathians, buffeted by the bitter winds of Russia. And yet, as Lilias observed, *"Inwardly it was all aglow, as I never knew a place to be in all my life—on fire with a spirit of sacrifice that did not even know itself to be sacrifice, it is so the natural expression of love."*

It had been a small mission outpost, until the time of the Welsh Revival when Sister Eva's lifelong search for God was met *"by a full drought from His fountain."* The mission grew from a staff of 24 to 150 "sisters," the household numbering 300, including orphans, students, infirmed villagers, babies—to say nothing of other related ministries.

It was the music from the orphan children—*"like birds singing in the dawn"*—that awakened Lilias every morning and set the course of gladness for the rest of the day. What an inspired ending to the rigors of a speaking ministry and renewal for the relaunch of ministry in Algiers.

Music. "Music is well said to be the speech of angels," wrote Thomas Carlyle, "in fact, nothing among the utterances allowed to man is felt to be so divine." How does one explain the mystery of matching pitch with rhythm, to make a pleasing melody? Or pairing pitches to that tune—adding, perhaps, percussion or horn or strings—resulting in glorious harmonies? How is it that the experiencing of music transcends the physical sense of hearing or the neurological complexities of the brain, penetrating to the deepest places of the soul?

Little matter the simplicity or complexity: a single line of monastic chant … a simple hymn tune chorded with four notes and linked with text … a haunting folk song accompanied with a six-string acoustic guitar … the plaintive melodies of American spirituals … wordless music—a sonata, a symphony. Or put it all together—stage, actors, song, libretto, orchestra—into complex operatic form. "The twelve notes in each octave and the varieties of rhythm offer opportunities that all of human genius will never exhaust," noted Igor Stravinsky.

Many people, like myself, can trace key moments in life through particular songs or music associated with those events. Music captures the emotional essence of an experience that can only, with difficulty, be put into words.

Three such incidents immediately come to mind: two were in Israel although separated by many years; one was in a boat, on the Sea of Galilee. My husband and I were "alone" together, separated from family and friends, the overcast skies and choppy water matching my mood. Then from another section of the boat, a group of travelers launched into song: the words of a beloved old hymn, "Dear Lord and Father of Mankind," to an unfamiliar but compelling tune. The clear voices in lilting English accent wrapped the threads of sound around my heart, uniting the Church Universal, here in Israel, in their England, and in my own USA:

> *Drop Thy still dews of quietness till all our strivings cease;*
> *Take from our souls the strain and stress,*
> *And let our ordered lives confess the beauty of Thy peace.*

The second "Israel Experience" was in the Jewish Quarter of the Old City. I heard the heartrending music of a string quartet before I saw them: four gentlemen seated on folding chairs, in an open space within the cloistered walkway—instrument cases open to receive the chance token of appreciation. They had been members, I learned, of a famed Russian orchestra, now refugees piecing together a living—their price for freedom.

Most recently music connected me across the miles, via phone, with my mother who was finding less to talk about as her world became smaller. And yet! She would come alive when I would recall a beloved song—some from her early camp meeting years—and together we would sing those texts of affirmation, she filling in where I would forget the words. "Leaning on the Everlasting Arms." "Great Is Thy Faithfulness." "Come, Ye Disconsolate."

Music touches places in the heart when words alone fail. It comforts and consoles. Music expresses thoughts unutterable. "Music is the shorthand of emotions," Tolstoy proclaimed, conveying emotion for which words are inadequate. "Music," according to Dietrich Bonhoeffer, "will help dissolve your perplexities and purify your character and sensibilities and in time of care and sorrow will keep a function of joy alive in you."

I clean house to the lyrical music of Mozart and worship to the hymn lines of Isaac Watts and Charles Wesley. Soulful tunes—folk songs and spirituals and gospel music and Vaughn Williams's arrangements—fill my heart. A catchy foot-tapping tune from a popular score or praise chorus invariably lifts my spirits. And from time to time I devote an entire evening to a concert beautifully staged and orchestrated with perfect acoustics. Still the sweet song of a child (grandchild!) catches me unexpectedly with a jolt of joy!

Music! Who but God could have imagined such a gift?! The language of angels; the transport of mortals to the infinite.

God, You have filled Your world with birdsong, rushing wind, and the splashing of rain. You have gifted humankind with the skill to create sounds and songs. Speak to my soul through music and lift my heart in praise to You.

FEBRUARY FLOWERS

Great are the works of the LORD;
they are pondered by all who delight in them.

PSALM 111:2

*The spring flowers that stand all about my room in
Arab pots of green and yellow earthenware bring a very real revelation
of Him, "by whom were all things created." The clear happiness of
the daisies and the radiant shout of the celandines, and the deep
sweet joy of the great almond blossoms with their mystical hearts—all are
literal foreshadowing of the "gladness above His fellows."*

DIARY FEBRUARY 13, 1927

SPRING ARRIVES EARLY IN CENTRAL Florida. Sap pushing dead leaves from trees; buds swelling from branches, orange blossom scenting the air. Indications of new life abound: bud and leaf and frond.

> *Nothing is so beautiful as Spring —*
> *When weeds, in wheels, shoot long and lovely and lush;*
> *...*
> *What is all this juice and all this joy?*
> *A strain of the earth's sweet being in the beginning.*
> — GERARD MANLEY HOPKINS

Even as I savor each indication of new life—spring!—flower shops and grocery shelves are flooded with bulb flowers evoking for me the quiddity of my childhood. Spring flowers: narcissus, tulip, daffodil, crocus. A northern spring!

February flowers. Native beauty; northern nostalgia. Garden or green house. Little matter. Each speaks its special message through shape and texture and hue. Straight through the senses to the heart.

God spoke to Lilias through His Handiwork. Flowers were, for her, His intimate love letter. Each stage of growth, from bud to bloom to seed, was not only a source of delight but a message straight from God—"*a very real revelation of Him 'by whom were all things created.'*" Daisy … cyclamen … poppy … soldanella … dandelion … desert crocus … Each contained a special lesson. Each pointed to its Creator.

Lilias's early pocket sketchbooks captured, in watercolors, English wayside flowers and alpine wildflowers. Her first year in Algeria she painted flowers unique to North Africa along with vignettes of people and places, and later she recorded desert flowers of an even more exotic character. During her pilgrimage to Palestine, she observed: " … *Galilee—all in its spring beauty of flowers budding fig-trees—all our own North African flowers … & it brings a hallowing over our blossom time there to know that they have their sister flowers here & that they must have been dear to the Lord's eyes & heart*" (March 26, 1924).

While bound to bed, during her final years, she culled images of flora and fauna from forty years of loving—village, plain, desert—and locked them into the delicate paintings (along with people and places) that became the treasured publication *Between the Desert & the Sea*, her love affair with North Africa.

Lilias's classic work *Parables of the Cross* demonstrates through the life stages of plants and flowers how death is necessary for life to continue in the physical world—and in the spiritual:

> *"Death is the gate of life." Does it look so to us? Have we learnt to go down, once and again, into its gathering shadows in quietness and confidence, knowing that there is always "a better resurrection" beyond?*
>
> *It is in the stages of a plant's growth, its budding and blossoming and seed-bearing, that this lesson has come to me: the lesson of death in its delivering power. It has come as no mere far-fetched image, but as one of the many voices in which God speaks, bringing strength and gladness from His Holy Place.*

Flowers "speak" their own individual story: poppy … buttercup … dandelion … vetch. Like the *Parables of the Cross*, they speak of living, yes, but of dying as well. Dying in order to live, "*bringing strength and gladness from His Holy Place.*"

Thank You, God, for the ever-changing beauty of Your natural world. Speak to me through Your handiwork and renew me with Your fresh returns.

BOUND AND YET UNBOUND

But the man who looks intently into the perfect law that gives freedom, and continues to do this, not forgetting what he has heard, but doing it— he will be blessed in what he does.

JAMES 1:25

The milky looking glacier spoke with God's voice this morning—so obedient to its course in its narrow bed,—yet just—tossing with freedom & swing in every motion—such a picture of the rivers "of living water"—bound & yet unbound.

JOURNAL AUGUST 8, 1899

I LOVE IT WHEN LILIAS ministers to me—through other people. Such was my experience this week when I read a devotional that included a quote from Lilias. I looked up the quotation, in context, and discovered a painting of the same.

Subject? Obedience. A word most often associated with "rules"—one short (negative) step from restrictions. And yet, Lilias chose to illustrate "obedience" with a glacier "*tossing with freedom & swing in every motion.*"

Is that true? Is there, in fact, evidence (if not proof) of liberty within limits … freedom within boundaries …? Or, as Lilias stated, the paradox of being "*bound & yet unbound*"?

I look to my heroes of faith and find C. S. Lewis on my short list. Lewis was a man of faith with a lifestyle light years from mine: scholar (Oxford and Cambridge-based academician), single for most of his adult years, and British. Convicted of his need for a spiritual director, Lewis chose to place himself in a relationship of accountability—a decision challenged by his own innate "private" nature. His choice, Anglican priest Walter Adams, would have perhaps the most profound input on Lewis's development during his spiritually formative years.

Adams seldom missed an opportunity to remind people to "look after the roots and the fruits will look after themselves." Both Adams and Lewis agreed that the "deep watering of the roots required radical obedience to every thing the Lord required, regardless of how small or mundane it seemed." Lewis wrote: "Discipline is the key to all doors" (*Seeking the Secret Place: The Spiritual Formation of C. S. Lewis*, by Lyle Dorsett).

Letter writing was one such thing Lewis believed God required of him. If readers took the trouble to write to him, it was his inviolable obligation to respond to them whether to answer questions or respond to their gratitude. Little did he realize when he submitted to that discipline how, a decade later, he would be bombarded with mail, his writings and radio lectures having made him a household name. When questioned about this "bane of my life," he never veered from his original belief, "When Christ gives an order it must be done," even if he didn't fully understand why. While he understood the immediate value of any writing that "illuminated the heart," he didn't know what would become of these letters (many now in published "collections"): a spiritual legacy for generations to come.

The common perception is that "obedience" to some higher power or rule stifles freedom. Yet Lewis insisted: "Obedience is the road to freedom" (*Letters to Malcolm*). Life confirms the same. Consider the value of boundaries in art. Take the sonnet, for example, a poetic form with a fixed pattern of lines, meter, and rhyme. From this exacting structure has emerged some of the world's greatest poetry: Shakespeare's penetrating insight into human nature; Milton's profound resolution to his blindness; Elizabeth Barrett Browning's outpouring of passion and love. Thought compressed to crystalline hardness radiates with the clarity and brilliance of a diamond. The precision and power that makes these sonnets so compelling must be attributed, in part, to the defining refining role of restriction. One could go on and on with like illustrations in various disciplines: sports, science, music, for a start.

Back to point. These are only examples, in microcosm, of what God intended for us—lives rich and free and joy filled—when we live within His prescribed boundaries. He has given us a rulebook (Scripture) and a Guide (the Holy Spirit) to instruct us and inspire us.

Frankly, I really don't like to be told what to do. But what if I'm instructed by someone I really trust? What if it is for my good? My *highest* good? The obedience of which Lewis and Lilias wrote was, of course, to the God of the Bible. Can He be trusted? Does He have my highest good in mind? If so … surely I must "trust and obey," as summed in the old gospel song, "for there's no other way to be happy in Jesus …"

Like the glacier *"so obedient to its course in its narrow bed—such a picture of the rivers 'of living water'—bound & yet unbound!"*

Strengthen me, Lord, to embrace the obedience that leads to true freedom. May I experience the joy of living this day within the boundaries of Your will.

THE GLADNESS OF MY JOY

Therefore God, your God, has set you above your companions by anointing you with the oil of joy.

PSALM 45:7B

FRIDAY, AUGUST 4.   SATURDAY, AUGUST 5.

We speak of the God of Love and the God of Peace—
so seldom of the God of Joy. God is the God of joy, and we must drink
in the spirit of His joy. And flowers speak of the gladness that is in the heart of God.
Flowers are not a necessity—they are just an overflowing of God's gladness
and if we look closely at each, it seems to reveal His joy each in a different way.
"Thy Face the heart of every flower that blows." You can
read Him in them ... God the gladness of my joy ... the merry heart
of the celandines and the pure simple happiness of the primrose and the shout
of the daffodils' golden trumpet. He didn't promise us ease and
comfort—but He did promise joy which we may have in the midst
of any weight or heaviness that may be ours to bear.

NOTES FROM LILIAS'S STUDY ON THE
TEMPLE CARVINGS JULY 17, 1928

THESE WORDS ABOUT JOY WERE penciled faintly in Lilias's final entry of her journal: July 17, 1928. They were notes for Sunday afternoon Bible readings, based on the carvings on Solomon's temple, during the lull of the summer when most of the workers took their much-needed breaks. The remaining few gathered around her bed for what would be her last meditations on earth. The next month, on August 27, she would be "Home" for *her* well-deserved rest.

Joy was a common theme woven throughout the pages of her diaries and her life. Friends testified to the same, quoting Lilias: "Oh, we do need a real laugh sometimes, don't we?" And, "I wish so-and-so could laugh more," she said of a new worker, "but she'll shake free. They always do."

Clearly, she experienced daily all manner of concerns that fairly could be called "joy killers." Who can't relate to that? If only, we think … if only this person, this illness, this financial pinch, this situation could be altered—then I could be happy.

But the joy Lilias described was not determined by outward events or circumstances. It was the joy Jesus mentioned on His way to Calvary, promising His disciples "a full measure" of His joy and echoing the psalmist's declaration, "Your God has set you above your companions by anointing you with the oil of joy" (Psalm 45:7).

Joy stands in sharp contrast to happiness, which tends to be directly related to our circumstance: Christmas Day surrounded by family; a long-desired trip; acquisition of a longed-for house or car or object; a good medical report. Joy holds firm when all the above fails or falls away.

The joy of which Lilias spoke continues even when "happiness" fades, when the externals that buoyed our spirits no longer hold. This kind of joy runs deeper than all external prompts or perks. It is based on the deep and confident assurance of God's love and work in our lives. That He will be present no matter what! *He didn't promise us ease and comfort—but He did promise joy which we may have in the midst of any weight or heaviness that may be ours to bear.*

I trust you can think of someone who embodies that kind of joy—in Scripture (Paul!) and in your own personal network. I was privileged to have that modeled by my mother. She was not, by nature, a bouncy positive person. Her temperament was contemplative, even melancholic. What's more, I witnessed, through the years, her experiencing her own share of setbacks and discouragements.

And yet, in the very midst of personal and maternal battles, she chose to focus on the small joys amidst the big trials; she chose to see redeeming elements in troublesome days. She used occasions of doubt to remind us (and herself) of God's past faithfulness. During a given struggle, she celebrated life, often turning to her tea-tray set with a Lusterware pot, bone china plates and cups, silver spoons and tea strainer, and (when in season) a flower in a cut-glass vase, inviting us into the comfort of this ceremony. Her legacy, in part, was her example of "living above the circumstance."

I have all of the above now—her tools of trade—and I also have the "inside story" in her journals: records of hard days as well as glorious. It all rings true: even as she records with heartbreaking accuracy the struggles of her everyday life, she rejoices in all manner of beauty that surrounds her—nature, family, and, yes, tea time—and gives witness to her confidence that God will not forsake her or hers.

So, I move forward, secure in the confidence that my emotional barometer need not be determined by circumstances, which change like the weather, but in an unchanging God—who is the gladness of my joy!

God, let me sense the gladness of Your joy that transcends the circumstances of this day.

GLAD IN THE PRESENT DAY

*This is the day the L*ord *has made;*
let us rejoice and be glad in it.

PSALM 118:24

*You are right to be glad in His April days while He gives them.
Every stage of the heavenly growth in us is lovely to Him.
He is the God of the daisies and the lambs and the merry child hearts!
It may be that no such path of loss lies before you; there are people like the lands
where spring and summer weave the year between them, and the autumn
processes are hardly noticed as they come and go. The one thing
is to keep obedient in spirit, then you will be ready to let the
flower-time pass if He bids you, when the sun of His love
has worked some more ripening. You will feel by then that to try to keep
the withering blossoms would be to cramp and ruin your soul.
It is loss to keep when God says "give."*

PARABLES OF THE CROSS

SUCH A BEAUTIFUL AUTUMN DAY! I sit on a rocking chair and savor the view from our front porch: blooms of purple, red, magenta, pink—bush and border, arbor and window box—a kaleidoscope of color. Butterflies flutter above lantana lured by their blossoms of yellow and orange. White billowy clouds scuttle across a china-blue sky. A bright red cardinal darts from tree to fence to tree. The air is alive with bird song and the peck, peck, pecking of—a woodpecker! My heart fairly bursts with the joy of it all. October in Florida.

And my heart fills with gratitude for the dear clapboard cottage that shelters us, fitted with furnishings from our past homes, augmented now with treasured objects from parents and grandparents. Photographs and paintings and pictures mix with objects of sentiment—artifacts of family and friends. Just "things," yes, but things rich with heritage and memories—bridges connecting us to people and places ever dear to us.

I ask: do these things mean too much to me? Is it "right" to care so much for what, at best, is transient? I remember asking that same question several decades ago. We had just moved in to an old manse newly refurbished by the church. I would walk through the large rooms with high ceilings, hardwood floors, walls and trim freshly painted in *my* colors. I would savor my view of pond and park and live oak trees—and wonder: Is it right to love it so completely? It didn't help that at that very time I was working my way through Dietrich Bonhoeffer's *Letters and Papers from Prison*!

It was from those same letters, as it turned out, that I was given a perspective that informed me then—and now. His parents wrote to him, during the Christmas season, expressing their angst in celebrating the season knowing that he was living in such miserable conditions. He responded:

> *We ought to find and love God in what He actually gives us; if it pleases Him to allow us to enjoy some overwhelming earthly happiness, we mustn't try to be more pious than God Himself and allow happiness to be corrupted by presumption and arrogance, and by unbridled religious fantasy which is never satisfied with what God gives. God will see to it that the man who finds Him in his earthly happiness and thanks Him for it does not lack reminder that earthly things are transient, that it is good for him to attune his heart to what is eternal, and that sooner or later there will be times when he can say in all sincerity, "I wish I were home." But everything has its time, and the main thing is that we keep in step with God.*

I believe that this is what Lilias meant, in essence, when she wrote of being *"glad in His April days."* She was speaking of the Christian life in its totality. She observes that it seems that, for some, the April days are seamless, *"where spring and summer weave the year between them, and the autumn processes are hardly noticed as they come and go."* Her advice, echoed by Bonhoeffer's decades later, is that we should enjoy them *"while He gives them."* After all, *"He is the God of the daisies and the lambs and the merry child hearts!"* (And, I might add, of birds and butterflies and bright blooming flowers!) April days, notwithstanding, *"The one thing is to keep obedient in spirit"* or, in Bonhoeffer's words, "the main thing is that we keep in step with God." Obedience. To "*be ready to let the flower-time pass if He bids.*"

In reality, most of us *do* experience winter, January days, figuratively speaking, sometimes for long stretches of time, with only a sprinkling of April days to brighten the spirit atmosphere. And it may be the memory of "flower times" past that sustains us, that gives us hope for better days to come.

Back to my rooms, my views … my April day in October. It is "*right to be glad in His April days while He gives them*"—be it a succession of days, a short April season, or an April moment.

But I must hold lightly these very things that gladden my heart, today. I must embrace them as He intended: pointers to God, a glimpse of glory, a preview of heaven!

Lord, may I delight in all the blessings that gladden my heart today. May I hold lightly the same knowing that they are but a glimpse of glory that points to You.

IMAGES OF God

THE DEW OF THE SPIRIT

For our light affliction, which is but for a moment, worketh for us a far more exceeding and eternal weight of glory.

2 CORINTHIANS 4:17 KJV

The grass has to stand very still as it holds its precious "weight of glory"—and so has the soul on whom the dew of the Spirit comes. Literally, as easily as this dew, His dew is brushed off—some of us know it to our cost. An impulse of impatience, a sense of hurry or worry allowed to touch us, a mere movement of the self-life against His checking and He is gone, and our soul stands stripped and bare. Noiseless must be His Holy Habitation within us.

DIARY JUNE 30, 1885

FIVE WOMEN (ONE VIA CONFERENCE PHONE!) meet for four days united in singleness of purpose. We have chosen a place, set apart, free from routine activity. The old-world charm and natural beauty of the historic inn promises the possibility of refreshment of body and of spirit.

We know what we hope to accomplish: to explore broader venues to present and access the unique legacy of Lilias Trotter: art ... writing ... life ... We agree to the importance of her contribution—spiritual, artistic, ministry—during her lifetime and recognize its significance in our own lives. We believe her to be relevant today, to people aching for reasoned spiritual clarity, role models, and meaning beyond themselves.

What we don't know is how and where God wants to use her—or us. So we come humbly before God, seeking to ascertain and obey His bidding. Toward that end, we dream and discuss and deliberate, then stand back, so to speak, and release our thoughts to God's purposes. We search our hearts for our motives and for indication of anything that could possibly impede the work of God's Spirit in us and through us. Repeatedly. Throughout the week.

Home again, my new vision (beyond the task at hand) is a renewed desire to be sensitive to "the dew of the Spirit." In a context solely devoted to a single purpose, we were focused and intentional. Continually (and in community) we returned to the stance of supplicant, conscious of anything that could brush off the dew of the Spirit. But back, now, to the fragmented reality of my daily life, it is so easy to forget. To become careless or indifferent or, dare I confess, disobedient.

Lilias looked to the dew-bearing blades of grass. Absolute stillness was requisite to hold its precious "weight of glory." The soul, on which the dew of the Spirit comes, likewise, must remain still and quiet. She observes how easily this "dew" can be brushed off: "*An impulse of impatience, a sense of hurry or worry allowed to touch us, a mere movement of the self-life against His checking.*"

"*Noiseless must be His Holy Habitation within us.*" Challenged by Lilias's life and words, I pray for stillness of heart—not only during those unique times when consciousness is heightened by commitment and community, but daily through personal desire and intention.

Spirit of the living God, fall afresh on me. —Daniel Iverson

 OUR GOD SEES

*Are not two sparrows sold for a penny? Yet not one of them will fall
to the ground outside your Father's care ... So don't be afraid;
you are worth more than many sparrows.*

MATTHEW 10:29, 31

Today's story is a very pretty one. The little pickle Melha went right up to her nearly blind father and pointed to one of the pictures on the wall—one of the Lord calling a little child to Him—and said, "Look at Jesus." "I have no eyes O my daughter—I cannot see," was the answer. The baby thing lifted head and eyes to the picture and said, "O Jesus, look at father!" Was that not a bit of heavenly wisdom?

DIARY JULY 28, 1909

THE BEST-SELLING BOOK *LETTERS TO GOD* was published in 1991, delighting a readership with children's directness, humor, and startling clarity of expression. For example, "Dear God, I do not think that anybody could be a better God. Well I just want you to know but I'm not just saying that because you are God already. Charles." Perhaps more compelling, personally, are those candid conversations that arise spontaneously in the context of everyday living. Just as I treasured my own children's observations about God, now I relish accounts of *their* children's observations. ("Write them down," I warn my adult children. "You'll be surprised what you'll forget.")

An eight-year-old Kiersten, hiking a rocky hill, clasping her mother's hand as they climbed the steep terrain: "You are like Jesus to me—holding my hand and helping me. I feel safe with you."

A conversation overheard between six-year-old Davis and his four-year-old sister. "Audra, did you know that God can juggle houses?!" A nonchalant Audra, "Yeah, I know."

Children played an important role in Lilias's life. During her early years in Algeria, Lilias discovered that relationships with children gave her entrée to Arab families. Little gifts of bonbons for the children and pincushions for their mothers never failed to open their houses and their hearts. Later, through the decades, a parade of little girls came in and out of their home: some taking up permanent residency, others finding a bed off the street for the night. The pages of her diaries, illuminated with sketches and paintings, provide whimsical and tender vignettes of these irrepressible scamps, bringing joy (and challenges!) with their merry presence and disarming insight.

Little Melha was one such child. A wild bit of a girl, with dark eyes and long black lashes, she continually beguiled Lilias and her colleagues with her quaint ways and wise observations. With her simple request, "*O Jesus, look at father!*" she articulated a profound truth to her sightless father: the presence of an all-seeing God. So often a child receives in trust what we adults labor to believe. How can God possibly see us all at once? How can He keep everything within His sight or care? We attempt to reason out a mystery that confounds and transcends our human understanding. Yet throughout Scripture, this is affirmed: "The eyes of the Lord are everywhere" (Proverbs 15:3). "Nothing in all creation is hidden from his sight" (Hebrews 4:13). And "My eyes will watch over them for their good" (Jeremiah 24:6).

Perhaps that is why Jesus gathered children to Himself and upheld them as an example: "Let the little children come to me, and do not hinder them for the kingdom of God belongs to such as these. I tell you the truth, anyone who will not receive the kingdom God like a little child will never enter it" (Mark 10:14–15). Certainly a logical God did not intend to frustrate our minds with inconsistency and illogic. At the same time, the created can never presume to fully comprehend the mind of the Creator. C. S. Lewis observed in *Mere Christianity*, "That is one of the reasons I believe in Christianity. It is a religion you could not have guessed. If it offered us just the kind of universe we had always expected, I should feel we were making it up. But, in fact, it is not the sort of thing anyone would have made up. It has just that queer twist about it that real things have."

An older couple, much afflicted by ill-health and immobility, was asked the secret of their bright hopefulness. Without hesitation the wife answered, "His eye is on the sparrow, and I know He watches me." Civilla Martin went home that evening and penned the verses of a simple gospel song, concluding with this joyful refrain: "I sing because I'm happy, I sing because I'm free, / For His eye is on the sparrow, and I know He watches me."

Lord, You love children and uphold them as an example. Help me to accept the mysteries of faith with childlike trust in You.

 # SAFE AM I

*Can a mother forget the baby at her breast
and have no compassion on the child she has borne?
Though she may forget,
I will not forget you!*

ISAIAH 49:15

*As a mother comforts her child,
so will I comfort you.*

ISAIAH 66:13

lose no
more ti[me]
prayer
a
in Alger style —

Can you not remember, my sister, as if it were yesterday, the hour your first born child lay in your arms and how your heart glowed with such love and joy that all you suffered in bearing it to life was forgotten. And as it lay there, weak and helpless, its very need called to you all the time, so that you could not forget it for a moment because of the great fountain of loving care that had sprung up in your heart. Even in the night you would wake at its faintest cry, and put your arms round and care for its needs.

God created in you, my sister, that wonderful Mother heart, and He loves you with the same tender love that He has given you for your little ones, only far more tender and deep ... you have a place of refuge in God as safe and warm and beautiful as you have ready for your child. Come and hide your head there when you are afraid of what may happen and if you are troubled bring your troubles there as your children come to you.

HEAVENLY LIGHT ON THE DAILY PATH
(PRIVATELY PUBLISHED DEVOTIONAL FOR ARAB WOMEN)

ONCE AGAIN, WE EXPERIENCE THE high point in the year family-wise, as we gather with our children and grandchildren, twenty-one strong, for seven wonderful days at the beach. It doesn't take long for the cousins to reconnect after a year's absence and reestablish relationships in various configurations. Soon relaxed vacation routines emerge: long hours at the beach … late meals (lunches on the wrap-around porch, family dinners cooked, in turn, by each family unit) … evening family time … adult time (children bedded) when we talk late in the night (morning!) and share our stories of the year past.

It never ceases to amaze me how the children fill the sunny hours of the day, fueled by boundless energy and limitless imagination, beach and ocean providing the stage for play. I'm fascinated by shifting alliances—older children organizing activities … younger children wandering off to build a sand castle or chase a crab … the boys spending endless hours riding the surf … Adults offer structure and the occasional verbal directive ("you're out too deep"; "let's put on more lotion"; "it's time to eat"; "be gentle with little Addie") as a background to the child-generated activity.

Until—there is a crisis! Stings from a jellyfish … legs and arms attacked by sand fleas … hurt feelings … an unresolved argument … possession rights challenged. Then cousins are instantly abandoned. The wounded child rushes to its parent, usually to a mother's lap. Often the comfort of a listening ear or a hug and kiss or a Band-Aid is sufficient, and a child is off and running again.

Lilias, ever seeking to find means to convey spiritual verities to the Arab women, seized on the maternal relationship to illustrate the heavenly Father's love in her self-published booklet *Heavenly Light on the Daily Path*. Illustrated with simple line drawings, she borrowed from the common, homely activities to illuminate heavenly truths: Writing in "The Lesson of the Mother's Lap": "*God created in you, my sister, that wonderful Mother heart, and He loves you with the same tender love that He has given you for your little ones, only far more tender and deep.*" She underscored that truth with the Scripture passage of Isaiah 49:15 and Isaiah 66:13.

No less do we, as adults, need the comfort and reassurance of a heavenly Father. Nor are we, like our children, beyond the reach of our heavenly Father. We may be more sophisticated than our children in how we view our world, our expectations about God having been shaped by life experience and observation. We may not believe that all will turn out as we want, but rather understand that no matter what happens God will be there with us.

The challenge to convey, and accept, a personal and loving God was not unique to Lilias and her beloved Arab friends. Julian of Norwich (1342–1416) wrote *Revelations of Divine Love*, tender meditations on God's eternal and all-embracing love: "God is our clothing, who wraps and enfolds us for love, embraces us and shelters us, surrounds us with his love, which is so tender that he will never abandon us." She concludes her meditation with the reassurance that despite all the trials and sorrows faced by God's creation, in the end "all shall be well." All shall be well, because God constantly enfolds His creatures in His constant upholding love.

I look at our grandchildren, even our adult children, for that matter. How I long to embrace them, figuratively speaking, in my "mother lap"—to shield and shelter them from the inevitable sorrows of life. Yet I know that they will experience setbacks and suffering that no Band-Aid or hug or listening ear can assuage. Better by far to point them to their heavenly Father who is present for them in this world and will usher them safely into eternity.

A song they learned in Bible school—by Mildred Leightner Dillon—comes to my mind, replete with motions—hand covering a cupped palm: "Safe am I (safe am I) in the hollow of His hand."

Adult. Child.

You have a place of refuge in God—safe and warm and beautiful ... Come and hide your head there when you are afraid of what may happen and if you are troubled bring the trouble there ... when Satan tempts you or the world draws you run to your refuge ... if the night of death comes before Jesus returns He will take you in His arms and hush your soul to sleep and you will know nothing more till you wake in the new day of heaven.

Thank You, Lord, for Your tender care. Enfold me, and mine, in Your loving embrace.

# SEEKING SHEPHERD

*I myself will tend my sheep and have them lie down, declares the Sovereign L*ORD*.
I will search for the lost and bring back the strays. I will bind up the injured and
strengthen the weak ... I will shepherd the flock with justice.*

EZEKIEL 34:15–16

*I must put down a dear little story told me by a friend this morning.
Her small niece, aged somewhere between three and four, was heard telling
the parable of the lost sheep to a cousin a year or two older.
The finale was, "So the Shepherd put back the lamb into the fold,
and then He mended up the hole where it had got out." All of sanctification
as well as salvation lay in the wisdom of those child-lips!*

DIARY MAY 28, 1926

THE TRIPTYCH OF THE PARABLE of the lost sheep was drawn by Lilias during her early years in North Africa. She captures, in three frames, a sequence that illuminates the full story of the straying lamb.

Panel 1: The foolish little lamb escapes from the fold. Pert and confident it sets off—to who knows where—on its journey toward independence. With a world to discover, nothing impedes the adventure.

Panel 2: A drastic change in circumstance. Who knows how far the lamb has wandered or what he has experienced along the way. His plight is grim. Entangled in briars, he is completely at the mercy of the elements. There is no escape from the approaching serpent. The vulture circling overhead definitely is not a good sign. He is virtually without hope.

Panel 3: Saved! Scooped up into the arms of the shepherd! Not a trace of judgment is on his savior's face. We see only love looking down, with infinite tenderness, upon the obviously shaken lamb held close to his heart. The woolly head turns upward, gratefully gazing at the saving shepherd who, we note, wears a crown of intricately woven thorns.

The triptych depicts Jesus's parable of the lost sheep (Luke 15:1–7). It wordlessly conveys a threefold message: lost, sought, found. But to fully appreciate the story, one must understand the context. Two groups of people had gathered around Jesus: the "good guys" (Pharisees and synagogue teachers); the "bad guys" (tax collectors and sinners). The religious group is offended by the fact that Jesus is eating with the "sinners," table fellowship being a sign of acceptance and friendship. Jesus's answer to their complaint is oblique. He tells three stories about three lost things: a lamb, a coin, a son.

The parable of the lost lamb aptly describes the character of sheep and of the shepherd. Sheep, by nature, are dumb, directionless, and defenseless. "By their very nature they need a shepherd," writes Charles Spurgeon, "and I suppose this is another reason why the figure of sheep is used to describe the relationship between the Lord and His people." In contrast to the religious leaders who shunned the "sinner," the Good Shepherd set off to find him. Jesus's heart ached for sinners, knowing that they were, in truth, *lost*. The response to the lamb being found was to throw a party, one that reverberated in heaven! Jesus, the great Shepherd, makes the parallel: "There will be more rejoicing in heaven over one sinner who repents" (Luke 15:7).

The image of her heavenly Father as the loving shepherd was Lilias's favorite, the one to whom all her endeavors pointed. She was unceasingly drawn to the "lost lambs," whether the prostitutes of London's Victoria Station, the street urchins of Algiers, the cloistered woman of the Casbah, or the mystic brotherhoods of the Southlands. Often she shared this picture with an individual to reassure them that whatever their situation, however grave their sin, they had a shepherd whose heart would seek after them and would rejoice when they were safely back in the fold.

Lilias used this simple picture to illustrate a life-proven truth. I have reproduced multiple copies of it, one framed and placed on a shelf along with other images of the Good Shepherd; the rest at the ready to assure a hurting heart of the love of the endlessly seeking Shepherd. For who of us has not ached for a "lost" child or family member or friend or neighbor? Who of us has not, at one time or another, been that lost lamb? We can take comfort in the heart of a seeking—and caring—Savior.

O God, whose Son Jesus is the good shepherd of your people: Grant that when we hear his voice we may know him who calls us each by name. —*Book of Common Prayer*

 SPRING OF LIFE

*I am the vine; you are the branches. If you remain in me
and I in you, you will bear much fruit.*

JOHN 15:5

*How does a branch that is not a branch become one? By grafting.
It must be severed from the plant on which it grew,
and the severed surface is brought to a wounded place
in the vine's stem, and bound there, heart to heart, and from the wounded
place in the stem the sap flows out and seals the branch into union,
and then it finds its way into the channels of the graft, and soon it needs
no outward bonds to bind it there: it has become one with the vine.*

THE SEVENFOLD SECRET

IT WAS JESUS, REALLY, WHO put this idea into personal terms the night before His crucifixion. John 15 relates an address to His disciples, in the upper room in which He draws them a beautiful word-picture of that relationship. But how, one might ask, can one that is a "branch" become one with the "Vine"?

This is a graphic picture for those of us who live in Central Florida, home of the citrus industry. Not long after we moved to Lake Wales, citrus growers informed me that Florida's orange crop is created from orange limbs grafted into native lemon root stock.

And so it is with the new life in Christ. We must be grafted into the vine that is Jesus. There is both a negative and positive aspect to such a union. Just as the old branch must be severed completely from its original source of life, we too must experience the "severance" from our "old life" through confession and repentance. However sharp and abrupt it may seem, we are ready for the grafting into the new life. We are bound to the vine, heart to heart, at the place where Jesus was wounded for us.

And this is just the beginning! As the sap flows freely from the vine to the branch, the Spirit of God flows freely into our hearts, through no effort of our own. Unless, of course, we clog or impede the flow by sin or indifference. "*It is utterly, unbelievably simple. Receive Jesus with a heart-grasp and you will find, like the flower, a spring of eternal life, entirely distinct from your own, set working deep down in your inmost being,"* Lilias wrote in *Parables of the Christ-life*.

What could be more desirable to a thirsty heart than an endless spring of life in one's inmost being, regardless of the parched or tired circumstances of one's outward existence?

The union is established, yes, but it is the beginning of new relationship, and like any relationship it requires nurture. Jesus concluded His teaching with a comforting implication of this new union: "I no longer call you servants … Instead I have called you friends" (John 15:15). Yes, we are joined in Christ, but now we have the unique privilege of abiding with Him, an ongoing process of knowing Him, of becoming more completely what He intended us to be: full persons. Whole.

I conclude where I began, with citrus, and a cautionary tale. For many years, after moving to Florida, I expressed my longing for a tangerine tree. It seemed to me the perfect fruit: sweet and accessible, the soft skin easily removed for instant enjoyment. One day, to my great joy, I discovered in a corner of our front lawn, yes, a tiny tangerine tree rich with the promise of future delights planted secretly (in the night?) by a good friend (and listener!) who was also in the citrus business. I watched it grow into a large symmetrical tree with glossy green leaves. It looked beautiful.

One day, several years later, said grower queried about my tree. "No fruit yet? Something's wrong with this tree." Then he threatened, "I'm going to smother the ground with fertilizer. If this doesn't work, I'm cutting it down."

I pled with him. I love this tree. It is beautiful. It provides shade and climbing for the children. He looked at me as if I were out of my mind: "That's all right for you to say. But I'm a citrus farmer. As far as I'm concerned, if it doesn't bear fruit, it's not doing its job. I'm cutting it down."

A happy ending to this story. It did bear fruit—for years and years. And it taught me a lesson. Citrus tree or branch, it exists to bear fruit: *the power and sweetness of the vine flow into the branch that has lost its own life to find it in the new life which flows on till leaves and flowers and fruit appear.*

Our true shelter and dwelling place is in Jesus, the eternal spring of life, who works within our inmost being. As we abide in that shelter, it becomes our true home, all the fibers of our heart locked in together with it, as the grafted branches abide in the vine, drawing from it the spring of life.

God, flow freely into my heart with Your life-giving Spirit. May I, unimpeded by sin and self, bear fruit to glorify You.

LESSON OF THE CRAB

*The Sovereign L*ORD *is my strength,*
he makes my feet like the feet of a deer,
he enables me to tread on the heights.

HABAKKUK 3:19

I had a beautiful day alone at Pescade, in a fresh little cave that we had never found before. My sermon was from a little crab perched on a rock below, which matched his light-brown shell exactly. He was just as alive and just as happy whether basking the air and sunlight—or buried (as took place about every other minute) under a foot or two of water as a wave swept over him. I could see him though the clear green-ness, quietly holding on below. There is no place where it is difficult for Jesus to live. His life in us can be just as adaptable as the life He has given to this tiny creature.

JOURNAL 1893

IT'S THURSDAY ALREADY, AND I have barely touched the projects intended for this week! Coming off the high of travel and family vacation and the elastic hours of summer, I was ready to press forward, this week, with a new and disciplined schedule.

The Plan: Address several back-burner writing assignments … tackle major household projects … catch up with my soul …

The Reality: Attend backed-up correspondence … sift and sort piles of accumulated papers … pick up bits and pieces of odds and ends (Fisher Price "people," doll boots and bonnets, and the remnants of grandchildren's creative play) … clear a refrigerator cluttered with three weeks' of unfinished food and drink … and more.

Now the day is half spent, and productive working time has been swallowed by activities that can't be tallied. I tighten with inward pressure as I recalibrate the schedule to salvage the remaining hours. I worry: Will I meet my long-range deadlines if I can't even keep up with the simple tasks of today?

Once again, I remind myself, it is not what I'm doing, or *not* doing, that defines the value of my work or worth. It is who I am—*whose* I am—amidst all the clutter and seeming unproductivity of a given day. Furthermore, it is less what I am doing and more *how* I'm doing the inevitable "next thing" on my limitless list of "to do's."

I almost skipped my time alone, today, with God. Surely He understands. I can still talk to Him (pray on the run, so to speak), I reasoned. Moreover, my Scripture reading for today is in Habakkuk! What does the gloomy prophet (a minor one at that!) have to say to me?! But pause, I did, and he spoke directly to my heart:

"*There is no place where it is difficult for Jesus to live.*" He is present whether I'm "*basking the air and sunlight,*" ticking off one important thing after another in a superproductive life, or "*buried under a foot or two of water,*" washed by waves of unfinished tasks outwardly or discouragement inwardly.

The key is to be attentive to God. Attentive to His leading … to His voice. He is present. Am *I*? He speaks. Am I listening? Or has all the din and clatter of my cluttered life muted His word and blocked His presence in my life? Wisdom of François Fenelon, from the seventeenth century, rings true today: "Be silent, and listen to God. Let your heart be in such a state of preparation that His Spirit may impress upon you such virtues as will please Him. Let all within you listen to Him."

There is no place where it is difficult for Jesus to live. His life in us can be just as adaptable as the life He has given the little crab—basking in air and sunlight or buried under a foot or two of water—*if we attend*. If we give Him room to live in us.

Just this week an event took place that commanded the attention of the most experienced or hardened journalists. Little did Antoinette Tuff know what another ordinary day as a bookkeeper at a Georgia elementary school would hold. But her heroic, clear-headed, compassionate dealing, single-handedly, with a deranged young man armed with five hundred rounds of ammunition calmed him into peaceful surrender, saving God knows how many lives of students, faculty, and police. Within twenty-four hours she was a proclaimed heroine in a personal telephone conversation with the president of the United States.

Admitting her inner terror—"I was actually praying in the inside. I was terrified but I was praying"—she walked through this event, a prime-time featured guest with CNN's Anderson Cooper, whose questions drew her to her pastor's Sunday sermon about being anchored in the Lord and His Word.

Would her story have had a different outcome had she not been "anchored"—rooted and grounded—in the Lord? Her life, by her own public admission, was not without challenges "devastating" in nature. But she was a vessel God could use for purposes she could not divine.

What about me? What am I missing when I keep plunging ahead with my frenetic activities—too busy, too distracted to attend? What might God be able to do with my life—with *any* life—if only we listened to and attended His voice, anchored in Him?

In his book of the same name, Richard Foster describes the place where Jesus lives as a "sanctuary of the soul." He says, "Throughout all life's motions—balancing the checkbook, vacuuming the floor, visiting with neighbors or business associates—there can be an inward attentiveness to the divine Whisper. The great masters of the interior life are overwhelmingly uniform in their witness to this reality … We bring the portable sanctuary into daily life."

There have been many reminders this week, amidst the clamor and clutter of living, to cultivate that place "for Jesus to live," through times set aside, when possible and when not, to allow Him room to adapt within me, in the "portable sanctuary" of my heart.

Ever-present God, may I be attentive to Your presence. Come into the sanctuary of my heart and guide me in the actions and interactions of this day.

 THE PRICE OF POWER

For to be sure, he was crucified in weakness, yet he lives by God's power. Likewise, we are weak in him, yet by God's power we will live with him in our dealings with you.

2 CORINTHIANS 13:4

Two glad Services are ours,
Both the Master loves to bless:
First we serve with all our powers
Then with all our helplessness.

Those lines of Charles Fox have rung in my head this last fortnight—
and they link on with the wonderful words "weak with Him."
For the world's salvation was not wrought out by the three years in which He went
about doing good, but in the three hours of darkness in which He hung, stripped
and nailed, in uttermost exhaustion of spirit, soul and body—till His
heart broke. So little wonder for us if the price of power is weakness.

DIARY OCTOBER 27, 1924

AN ARMFUL OF FRESH FLOWERS—"*THE wonderful deep crimson vetch that the French say first grew on Calvary*"—inspired Lilias to capture a single sprig in watercolor. Her exquisite painting prompts my reflection on the account of Christ's impending death: what if He had lived a longer life on earth? Think of all the good He accomplished in three years of ministry. Healing the sick … feeding the hungry … restoring dignity to the outcast … raising the dead … meeting the human heart at its point of need … Think of the host of people who could have been touched by His hands and His heart. Imagine the sheer number of people who would have rallied to His kingdom purposes.

Fact is, during His years of ministry, Jesus continually played down His power, discouraging people from broadcasting His works or acclaiming His name. He even silenced the three disciples who witnessed His celestial glory in the Transfiguration. It was not until the glory seemingly had passed and He appeared most vulnerable that Christ spoke, acknowledging explicitly His kingship and implicitly His divinity. Walter Wangerin in his Lenten reflections, *Reliving the Passion*, challenges: "Christian, come and look closely: it is when Jesus is humiliated, most seeming weak, bound and despised and alone and defeated that he finally answers the question, 'Are you the Christ?' Now, for the record, yes: I *am*. It is only in incontrovertible powerlessness that he finally links himself with power: 'And you will see the Son of man seated at the right hand of Power.'"

Yes, He could have lived longer. Despite the furor created by His very presence, God could have stayed the onslaught of His enemies. After all, God is all-powerful. Omnipotent.

The overruling reality remains: The central purpose of Christ's mission on earth was to die. Without His death there could be no resurrection life, for Him, for us. Without Good Friday there would be no Easter. "*The price of power is weakness.*"

All the good He did on earth, even at the height of His greatness (as we assess greatness) didn't compare with what He accomplished at the apparent point of defeat. It can be said without the slightest trace of exaggeration: "*The price of power is weakness.*"

What does this say to the so-called sanctified view of power often held by the church signified by size, structure, and program? More to the point, what does it say to *me*? Surely God asks—and blesses—service given from our strength: the fruit of all our powers. Stewardship. But perhaps an even greater service, one He especially blesses with His love and His power, is born out of our helplessness. Weakness.

Paul's challenge to the early church, beginning with Christ's incarnation and culminating at the cross, holds to this very day:

Have the same mindset as Christ Jesus:
    Who, being in very nature God,
    did not consider equality with God something to be used to his own advantage;
rather, he made himself nothing,
    by taking the very nature of a servant,
    being made in human likeness.
And being found in appearance as a man,
    he humbled himself
    by becoming obedient to death—
    even death on a cross!

PHILIPPIANS 2:5–8

So little wonder for us if the price of power is weakness.

God, You know my inadequacy in the face of formidable challenges. Please meet my weakness with Your strength.

IMAGES
OF
Redemption

HARBINGER OF SPRING

See, I am doing a new thing!
Now it springs up; do you not perceive it?

ISAIAH 43:19

The long hard winter has broken at last—not as yet in much sign on the earthward side but in the late afternoon yesterday the great cumulus clouds sank away, and in their place lay long horizontal bars, one above the other, dove-grey touched with pale apricot, upon the tender eggshell blue of the eastern sky. They are a harbinger of spring out here, that I have never known to fail.

DIARY JANUARY 24, 1927

SPRING RETURNS TO CENTRAL FLORIDA. Or at least first signs of the same. While one could hardly call it a "hard long winter," compared to much of our country, there definitely has been a period of dormancy punctuated with stretches of chill even in our subtropical clime. So it is with a lift of joy that we welcome signs of new life—"harbingers of spring"—that signal new beginnings: tight new buds on our rose bushes, trees leafing out forcing off last season's remnants of withered leaves, grass filling in bare patches with green, a tiny yellow-bellied goldfinch flitting from branch to branch, trilling its song of praise.

And with spring comes a sense of renewal. The return of green and budding flowers brings a freshness of spirit and renewed energy. Some, like my mother, welcome spring with a brisk full-blown housecleaning, attic to basement, emptying bookcases and dusting each book, scrubbing walls and woodwork, washing windows and putting up screens, even switching out heavy drapery for gauzy organdy curtains to billow in the sweet spring breeze. Then the big finish: placing rich soil in old window boxes and filling them with young plants and fresh greenery.

I wonder if God intended the cycle of seasons to trigger within our spirits a like renewal. George Herbert in his beloved poem "The Flower" wrote: "How fresh, O Lord, how sweet and clean / Are thy returns! ev'n as the flowers in spring," suggesting that the same "returns" of His creation—"flowers in spring"—are possible in the souls of His creatures.

Surely God purposed us to see Him through His design—much as we see the artist through his or her consummate work, be it a building, a painting, a quilt.

One of the perks of researching the life of Lilias has been "conversations"—phone, e-mail, letter— with the few remaining people who knew her or knew people who did. Today I had yet another conversation with a woman in London who, with her husband, are the only living members of the original Algiers Mission Band. While they came to Algeria several decades after the death of Lilias, they lived in her home, Dar Naama, in the suburbs of Algiers. They worked with people who knew Lilias intimately, having served alongside her for many years.

At the end of our conversation, I put down my list of questions, and asked: "What would you like to tell me about Lilias? What would you want people to know?" She quickly said, "Love. Lilias was loved by the Arab people, and they knew that their 'La La Lily' loved them. But you can't talk about Lilias without noting her love of beauty, of nature. She rejoiced that God called her to a land of such beauty. And she believed that God's created order pointed back to the Creator—that we could learn about God through the beauty and design of His natural world."

"The world is charged with the grandeur of God," exulted Gerard Manley Hopkins. He notes humanity's ill-treatment of the earth but concludes:

And for all of this, nature is never spent;
    There lives the dearest freshness deep down things,
And through the last lights of the black West went
    Oh, morning, at the brown brink eastward springs —
Because the Holy Ghost over the bent
    World broods with warm breast and with ah! bright wings.

The rhythms of nature—night followed by day, the predictable seasons of each year—provide renewal and fresh starts in the physical world. They also suggest the same in the world of the spirit. Even as we open the windows of our houses to receive a fresh spring breeze, we can open the doors of our hearts to the refreshment that comes from the sweet breath of the Holy Spirit: *His* "nature never spent."

We know the bit of housecleaning our souls require, the refurbishing of our minds, the planting of new life in the spirit. Let us turn off our smart phones, take off our headphones, and be attentive to the world around us. What does God want us to see? What "new thing" does He want to do in our lives?

> *The day is yours, and yours also the night;*
> *you established the sun and moon.*
> *It was you who set all the boundaries of the earth;*
> *you made both summer and winter.*
>
> PSALM 74:16–17

God, Your world gives constant testimony to Your design: renewal and rebirth throughout the changing seasons of the year. Renew and refresh my soul with the sweet breath of Your Spirit.

# GLIMMER OF LIGHT

Let your light shine before men, that they may see your good deeds and praise your Father in heaven.

MATTHEW 5:16

*In the garden there is an African "soldanella"—not a real soldanella—
only an African version of the same truth of the wonders that God can
do in secret. A garden border of a kind of thick matted grass,
a foot high—so matted that the leaves were bleached yellow-white
for want of sun, for a full third of their length. But right down below
that level—almost on the ground—with barely a ray of light, its berries had ripened
to wonderful sapphire blue-like jewels when one parted the mass and came upon
them. Oh our God can do the same miracles with this tiny glimmer of light that comes
to these souls in their tangle of darkness. Glory be to His name!*

DIARY MARCH 17, 1904

IT HAD BEEN A DIFFICULT two and one half years for Lilias. Many of the advances in ministry had been curtailed by the French government's official resistance to all things English. On top of this was a sustained period of *"failure in sleeping powers & a sudden sense of having come to the end of my strength."* Her return from her summer retreat in England to her beloved Algeria had been repeatedly postponed, and, even now back in Algiers, she lamented her "idleness." (The definition of which could be contested, given the various projects with which she was engaged!)

Perhaps her deepest discouragement was the setback in hopes for a station in Tolga, a Southland village where in 1900 they had been received with warm hospitality and open hearts. They returned two years later, greeted with the same welcome, and purchased a house for a winter station. Their delight was boundless as they furnished their own native home—with earthen walls and floor, ceiling of palm trunk and thatch of palm leaves—and received a steady stream of visitors. Then, without advance notice, their work was shut down by the French military commandant: " … *our hopes for steady work down here wrecked at a stroke—we fairly ached, body and soul, with the blow.*"

The one bit of encouragement came, without any outward sign of confirmation, through the "post" (an Algerian rider on horseback)—a passage from Proverbs, with the marginal note, "Surely there will be a sequel," which became a promise Lilias claimed of God. "*A glimmer of light.*" And she praised God for what she could not yet see.

In the city of Algiers, Lilias carried on the ministry, limited in her estimation, but formidable by any other standard: writing story parables in native phraseology; translating portions of the New Testament in colloquial Arabic, recruiting new workers from the Training Center in nearby Olivage.

It was here, at Olivage, that she observed the African "soldanella" with its brilliant blue berries surviving, even thriving, under improbable circumstances: hidden from the sun under thick matted grass. And, once again, God spoke to her through His creation. It spoke of the wonders God can do in secret … of the miracles God can do with a tiny glimmer of light.

It would be another twenty-one years before Lilias would witness the "sequel" she believed God had promised. Her return to the Southlands, first through the desert gates of El Kantara and then to the mud-walled town of Tolga, touched her heart as it had so many years before: "*Everywhere in the streets there are hands stretched out in welcome—gaunt hands of old men who were in their prime then, strong brown hands of middle-aged men who were but lads when we saw them last.*" The mission home was reestablished. Lilias's love and vision for

Tolga never waned, and long after she was unable to make the journey to the Southlands, the ministry continued for generations.

Lilias's trust in God's working through the "glimmers of light" that penetrated the improbabilities of sight sustained her through countless ministry challenges. While few of us would compare our kingdom work with Lilias's radical ministry, the reality of God's working is the same. I believe and take heart from the spiritual insights she derived in the battle zones.

I wonder, from time to time, just what difference my small efforts have made in the bigger scheme of things. Particularly those that were limited by time or circumstances. The promising student I taught for a year, never to see again … individuals who peopled my life, for a moment, not to know what has gone on since … the self-contained mission trip or church program that consumed a week or so … the chance conversation concerning spiritual verities … even efforts extended to family members who might not have fathomed the cost.

You can add your stories, whether employed "full-time" in ministry or living out faith, full time. How much of your time and energy has been expended on people, projects, or simple acts of service without the slightest indication of completion or results? We touch a life, invest our souls only to move on or have them move away from us. How often are we frustrated by the magnitude of the task and the limits of our contributions?

Yet! It is not really about our shedding of light. It is what God is doing with that glimmer of light. Oh, the wonders God can do in secret!

This is confirmed in my own life when I consider the glimmers of light that illuminated my life, often for only a brief time, often unacknowledged by me: the woman who built a childhood library for me, book by book, until I was ten years of age, and we moved a thousand miles away; the Bible teacher who brightened my first year of college with hospitality (tea and cookies) and led us through the book of Ephesians; two third-grade public-school teachers who mentored me through my first year among them; the authors who shaped my faith; older moms who informed my view of parenting and homemaking; the two women who introduced Lilias to me and never knew what would evolve from their parting with their treasured books.

But I'm going to end where I started: with Lilias and the amazing "sequel" that prompted this reflection. Fast forward more than a century from the moment of despair when she claimed as from God "Surely there will be a sequel." Just this week I received an e-mail from a friend who met with a couple who had lived in Tolga! When she asked, "Have you ever heard of Lilias Trotter?" they answered a resounding yes. They had visited an Arab family in Tolga that mentioned a "Madame Lily" who had been a friend of their grandmother. This grandmother took classes from Madame Lily—food preparation and sanitation as well as needlework. She related how Lilias taught the girls to read—unheard of then—and even recalled Scripture verses that were since passed down through the generations. They credited her for modeling a tradition of hospitality for their family present to this day.

 Lilias had no idea what of her loving efforts would be remembered. Nor do we. But of this she was certain—and so can we—that God would work His wonders in secret … that He would do miracles with tiny glimmers of light.

 Lord, so much of my life is tending to little things with few obvious results. Take those tiny glimmers of light and work Your hidden wonders in the lives of others.

GOD'S WORKMANSHIP

For we are God's workmanship, created in Christ Jesus to do good works, which God prepared in advance for us to do.

EPHESIANS 2:10

*God builds up a shrine within us of His workmanship,
from the day in which Jesus was received. The seed-vessel is its picture.
With the old nature He can have nothing to do except to deliver it to death:
no improving can fit it for His purpose, any more than the leaf or tendril however
beautiful, can be the receptacle of the seed. There must be "a new creation,"
"the new man," to be the temple of the Divine Life.*

PARABLES OF THE CHRIST-LIFE

IT WAS THE SUMMER OF 1983. We were working our way up the eastern coast, stopping at B&Bs along the way, toward our destination: a family reunion on Cape Cod. As we were skirting Washington, D.C., Dave succumbed to my pleas to stop at the Washington National Cathedral. "Just one hour. Promise."—to fulfill my dream of seeing the then recently completed *Ex Nihilo* creation tympanum over the main doors of the west facade.

This sculpture had taken my heart from the first article I read about Frederick Hart's prize-winning design for the portrayal of the biblical creation. The eight "unfinished" figures emerging from stone, writhing with the agony of "being created," touched a deep place in my soul. It had been, for me, a challenging year on several fronts, and somehow this sculpture captured the very quiddity of the ongoing work of creation, making sense of what were, in reality, "trials" not "tribulations."

The children were only too glad to have an hour outside the confines of the car. Dave found a bench on which to read and nap. I was alone, on pilgrimage, and even if only for one hour, I was at liberty to study this masterpiece within a massive arch, towering above the great double doors of the cathedral.

It did not disappoint. Most compelling to me was the sculptor's vision of creation not as a finished work but as a process: a state of becoming. Evident in the figures and faces of force and beauty was struggle: bodies emerging out of the nothingness of chaos caught in a moment of transformation. Frederick Hart, in his own words, conceived his creation sculpture "as an eloquent metaphor for humankind always 'becoming,' ever in a state of rebirth and reaffirmation of all the possibilities in being human."

Time up. I purchased postcards of the creation tympanum, souvenir of these sacred moments and a reminder of the life-giving message inherent in those unfinished figures emerging from stone. Being created. *Becoming*. Years later I purchased a facsimile of the same, and mounted it over the lintel of our dining room doorway, under which I pass countless times a day.

Becoming. It might have taken the visual shock of seeing it demonstrated in stone to penetrate my dulled sensibilities, but it is a fundamental teaching of Scripture: "For we are God's workmanship, created in Christ Jesus to do good works, which God prepared in advance for us to do" (Ephesians 2:10). We are *being* created.

And in that recognition is both hope and caution. Hope: I am not a finished product. There's opportunity for improvement. Caution: It's not about *me*. It's not about me growing toward wholeness for random personal purposes or gain. We are being created "to do good works, which God has prepared in advance for us to do."

God, the master stonecutter, is continually at work, chipping and shaping His creatures into the beings He intended us to be. Some of the finished product is determined, at start, by the substance out of which we are being created. But the individuality, the specificity, is being determined by the skillful and purposeful hand of the Creator.

There is a limit, of course, as to how far one stretches the analogy. After all, unlike the soulless stone, we can resist the Sculptor's design. But there are many parallels to point out. The most obvious being, we did not make ourselves. We are the creation of something—Someone—regardless of the human processes that brought us into being. Second, while much of our growth occurs slowly, cell by cell, much shaping is requisite to make us fully formed human beings, reaching our full potential. Furthermore, much of the refinement of our *souls* has come as the result of the trials and testing that felt, at the time, like the sharp chisel of the stonecutter.

Speaking personally, I can look back over my life and acknowledge growth that came simply from the maturing process of age and experience. But, if I am completely honest with myself, my periods of greatest progress—*growth*—have come as a result of being tested and tried beyond my comfort zone: experiences that required more from me than I could personally resource; situations that ultimately (sometimes as a last resort) threw me into the arms of God. I would never choose the challenges or setbacks. Some hurt terribly, and I recoil from the blows. But I do have a choice to submit my life—with its inevitable challenges—into the hand of the Sculptor for His refining work.

In one of George MacDonald's books, a character named Dorothy proposes that a Mrs. Faber is "quarreling with the process" of God's craftsmanship. If only we would consent to the process, allowing the Creator to use the everyday joys and challenges for our formation, yes, but submitting to the chisel as well, knowing its sharp blows to be essential to the shaping of our souls—"*the temple of the Divine Life.*"

God's workmanship or ours? The choice is up to us!

God, I am Your workmanship, a work in process. Sculpt me into the person You intend me to be, to fulfill Your purposes for my life.

THE MYRRH OF HEARTBROKENNESS

Now you must repent and turn to God so that your sins may be wiped out that time after time your soul may know the refreshment that comes from the presence of God.

ACTS 3:19 PHILLIPS

som from it outside — inside we saw but
       to the darkness that it had

The gathering of the bitter-sweet myrrh of heartbrokenness over failure and short-comings—over all the "might-have-been's" of the past—can bring one nearer heaven than the gathering of frankincense of the hills, for present and future. Such is His abounding grace, even when sin has abounded. The place where we wash His Feet with our tears has a great nearness to His Holy place.

DIARY MARCH 14, 1926

I'M AN IDEALIST. I ADMIT it. Some might say a romanticist. I grew up with *Anne of Green Gables* and *Little Women* and built around myself an "idealized world" of beauty and goodness. And while I never was taught this bit of practical theology—much less worded it as such—it amounted to something like this: "If I do my best to live a good Christian life, if I cover each problem with prayer, God will spare me life's tragedies. Sure, I will face trials and testings (necessary for growth), but in the final analysis God will deliver those who love and serve Him." In short, a fairy-tale ending: "they lived happily ever after." Although this idea had its obvious flaws, it carried me through the ups and downs of childhood and well into my youth.

Then three crises converged, the summer between my sophomore and junior years of college, for which my Christian worldview was inadequate, crises involving death, financial reverses, and a life-changing family situation for a beloved cousin. Each situation touched my life deeply and had tremendous implications for all involved. And they all shared common ground: the fervent but seemingly unanswered prayers of godly people and irreversible damages—nothing gained (as far as I could see) but pain to all involved.

For the first time I was witnessing Christians with faith and experience far greater than mine go through situations that had no perceived happy ending. My first response was grief. For those I loved. For me—innocence lost. And then in time, grief was replaced with a kind of shadowy anxiety. How could I—how could *anyone*—be safe in a world that was not a respecter of persons?

Rare is the person who will sail through life without challenge. (Of course I was fortunate to have reached my late teens without having experienced significant trauma.) Sooner or later, there comes a time when the props that hold up our small crafts are insufficient. The death of a loved one. A betrayal. A physical disability. A personal failing.

The Bible is a story of broken dreams, dashed hopes, failures, and disappointments. Human failing is a thread running through the Old and New Testaments. But it is, above all, a book about redemption. God redeeming human failure, pain, and loss. It is the story of hope and fresh starts.

One of my favorite stories is about Joseph, who had more than his fair share of disappointments, betrayal, and setbacks. From Joseph, facing head on the very brothers who betrayed him, thus setting off the series of events that would ultimately lead him to being Pharaoh's second in command, we first hear these now-famous words: "You intended to harm me, but God intended it for good" (Genesis 50:20).

Isn't that the story of redemption? Taking something bad and turning it for good? Slavery for freedom: physical and spiritual. *Redemption* is a multifaceted word with many implications, but for much of my life I understood "redemption" as exclusive to salvation: once and for all, my sins were redeemed on the cross, Christ paying the cost, His life for mine.

And that, indeed, is a rich and fundamental doctrine of Christianity. But I've come to see that it is that—and more. God is *continually* involved in our redemption. He is in the business of an ongoing redemption in the life of each Christian, continually taking the bad and using it for good—if released to Him for that purpose.

What about those things that I have done wrong—from weakness or lack of intention or, worse, deliberation? What about actions or failings that may have long-term effects on others: my children, my friends? Looking back, I can see my mistakes, my failings, but what does one do when it is too late, when the damage—to myself or others—is beyond repair?

This story speaks, at slant, to questions in my heart: In the workshop of a great Italian artist, a young servant cleaned the studio every evening. One day he timidly asked, "Please, sir, would it be all right if I saved for myself the bits of broken glass you throw on the floor?"

"Do as you please; they are of no use to me."

For years the boy faithfully carried out his task. Every day he sifted through the discarded bits of glass, setting some aside.

One day the craftsman entered a back storeroom and came across a carefully hidden piece of art. Bringing it to the light and dazzled by its brilliance, he asked the servant, "What is the meaning of this? What great artist has hidden his masterpiece here?"

"Master," he replied, "don't you remember? You said I could have the glass you threw to the floor. These are the broken pieces" (adapted from *Mountain Trailways*, by Mrs. Charles Cowman).

God is the great redeemer of all circumstances. There is no situation resulting from either sin or ignorance that is beyond His reconstruction. While neither we, nor sometimes others, can escape the consequences of our actions, when we turn to Him with a humble heart, "*washing His Feet with our tears,*" and release to Him the shattered segments of our lives, He will take those broken pieces and make from them something good.

We cannot deny the existence of brokenness or the corresponding pain and hurt, yet there is nothing to be gained in staring at the broken pieces. Once we have, in true repentance, turned from our error, making every possible reparation, we must gather the fractured fragments and give them once and for all to the One who has promised to work all things for the good of those who love Him. The final design may not be what it would have been; the individual parts may be imperfect, yet the great Redeemer can take all the pieces and make from them a work of art excelling our human imaginings. "Redemption, in its deepest sense," wrote Alister McGrath in *Redemption,* "is about being accepted as we are, while being transformed into what we are meant to be."

"And we know that in all things God works for the good of those who love him, who have been called according to his purpose" (Romans 8:28).

God, You alone know the frailty and failures of my faithless heart. Please take the broken pieces, washed with tears of repentance, and redeem them for Your purposes.

BEAUTY FROM BROKENNESS

And we know that in all things God works for the good of those who love him, who have been called according to his purpose.

ROMANS 8:28

*Conscious weakness as a preparation for service is one thing;
brokenness is another. We may know that we are but earthen pitchers,
like Gideon's, with nothing of our own but the light within, and yet
we may not have passed through the shattering that sets the light forth.
It is an indefinable thing, this brokenness,
and it is unmistakable when it has been wrought.*

PARABLES OF THE CHRIST-LIFE

TWO PEOPLE E-MAILED ME AN article, "Beauty Restored." Both for the same reason. It reminded them of Lilias.

It was inspired by the *New York Times* op-ed article in which Angelina Jolie went public with her announcement of her preventative double mastectomy. The writer, Brian Draper, noted her bravery in "not hiding the scars of her own recent breakage and reconstruction." He went on to describe an ancient Japanese craft, *kintsugi*. When a valuable piece of china was dropped and broken, instead of throwing it away or repairing it, the craftspeople pieced it together with a lacquer mixed with gold. "And the restored item was considered far more beautiful than the original—because of its brokenness."

Brokenness. We live in a throw-away culture that denies or rejects imperfection. In things. In persons. Something breaks, we throw it away and replace it with something new. Some*one* is broken or imperfect. That person is shunned or sidelined, aborted or euthanized.

Yet no one is protected from or impervious to brokenness. At start, no one is born perfect. It is only a matter of time before something will mar any illusion we might have of perfection. Brokenness is our reality, regardless of cause: our own faults or failings … the result of another's abuse or carelessness, intentional or otherwise … or simply the reality of our existence in a broken world.

Indeed, it was into just such a broken world that Perfection came, taking on human form: to identify with us, to walk alongside us, to bear and heal our wounds, to be broken Himself, ultimately, in order to redeem and restore us. *Kintsugi*. Love is the gold-infused lacquer transmuting brokenness to wholeness and beauty.

Redemption: grace extended. Proof perfect that even in our very brokenness we are worth something. Worth restoring. *Kintsugi*. Thank God, He is not a deity with a throwaway mentality!

Lilias, in *Parables of the Christ-life,* refers to the Old Testament story of Gideon sending his men to battle, in the dead of night, equipped only with a sword and an earthen pitcher. Not until the pitchers were shattered could the candles within shine forth and illuminate their steps. In *A Path through Suffering,* Elisabeth Elliot noted, "The light is shed abroad because the vessel is broken."

Shattered. Broken. From that very brokenness God can make something of true beauty. We can choose to finger the fractured fragments of our lives scrutinizing them with self-reproach or bitterness. Or we can release them to God and view the emerging masterpiece being recreated by the skillful hands of the master craftsman.

God, we are broken people in a broken world. Take the brokenness of my life and heal it with Your life-restoring love.

# STORED ENERGY

He who began a good work in you will carry it on to completion until the day of Christ Jesus.

PHILIPPIANS 1:6

*There is something wonderful in the thought that all the world's
commerce of late, and much of the political movements
that stand co-related hang on the coal supply; in other words,
on bringing to the surface the buried lives of the trees and plants of ages far away.
May it not be that just as unlooked for results in ages to come may spring
from souls that "lay in dust, life's glory dead," and have before them
"a better resurrection" in power transmuted in undreamed of ways
when God's purpose come to birth. The buried fronds and fibres
seemed over and done with, but their stored-up sunrays were waiting
undimmed through those centuries on centuries of burial,
only waiting to be given out.*

I. LILIAS TROTTER, PIGOTT

POCKET SKETCHBOOK 1877

IT WOULD BE MORE RELEVANT, today, to use the analogy of "oil" to demonstrate the political and economic currency of buried energy, but the point is well taken even after one hundred years. Coal has been called "buried sunshine," because the plants that formed it captured energy from the sun to create the plant tissues and, in turn, carbon that gives most of its energy.

Lilias, as always, found lessons in nature that spoke to spiritual realities. Coal spoke to her of unlooked-for results from efforts of people from time past: "*'a better resurrection' in power transmuted in undreamed of ways when God's purpose come to birth.*"

I'll never forget the impact on those words when I first read them in Blanche Pigott's compilation of Lilias's letters and journals, *I. Lilias Trotter*. I was slowly—to make it last longer—working my way through the big brown book, savoring every bit of Lilias's wisdom and perspective. It came at a time when I was longing for encouragement that transcended the passing trends of conflicting methods and approaches to ministry. For that matter, approaches to *life*. As I read these life-giving trend-silencing words from a writer virtually unknown to me, I knew that God had gifted me this person from another time and place to speak eternal verities into my parched soul.

"*The buried fronds and fibres seemed over and done with, but their stored-up sunrays were waiting undimmed through those centuries on centuries of burial, only waiting to be given out.*" Her "sunrays" were buried only a century, in contrast to the possible millions of years needed to produce the "buried sunshine" of coal, but I felt at that moment that her words were "*waiting undimmed*" for this one needy person! Little could I then have imagined what "God's purposes" were for me concerning the "giving out" of that energy to others!

    Since then, I have thought often of this principle of stored energy from things (and people) past and present—for God's purposes in God's time. And it begs the question: what am I doing now that might have consequences for the future? We see this a bit with our progeny: in the normal course of events, our children will outlive us. We will never know fully the effects of our training and example on their lives or even their impact on others'. Perhaps we have consciously invested in something much bigger than ourselves: a church, a company, a building, a project, a work of art … We don't know the results of those efforts in a future with, or without, ourselves. It's a bit like Nelson Henderson's adage: "The true meaning of life is to plant trees under whose shade you do not expect to sit."

Sometimes this is easier to perceive with hindsight. I think of Werner Burklin, son of missionaries to China, who saw his parents' ministry shut down; under house arrest for five years, they were eventually forced out of the country. They would never know that, decades later, their son and then their grandson would return to the very province where they first lived, to provide leadership training and materials for countless Chinese pastors ministering to millions of national Christians. "*Stored-up sunrays waiting undimmed*" through the years "*only waiting to be given out.*"

Less spectacular, but no less providential, my husband and I have been privileged, throughout four decades of parish ministry, to witness individuals who late in life have come into a personal relationship with Jesus. Often, part of their story is an account of a parent or grandparent who prayed for them yet never knew of their commitment. "*Stored-up sunrays waiting undimmed through the years, only waiting to be given out.*"

Tree or coal notwithstanding, we are by nature creatures of the here and now: what you see is what you get. We live in a culture that craves and promotes instant gratification: You don't witness results? Move on to something more productive. Now.

But what have we missed when driven by results, alone? Is it possible that we've lost the bigger picture in which God wants us to play a significant, if unnoticed, part? Perhaps it comes, in part, from our limited understanding of time? In *Mere Christianity*, C. S. Lewis suggests that our concept of time is quite different from God's: "Almost certainly God is not in Time. His life does not consist of moments following one another … every other moment from the beginning of the world—is always the Present for Him … He has all of eternity in which to listen."

Lilias, as much a strategist as she was, acted fully in the present, listening and waiting on God to do His bidding. She left the "results" to Him. "His time, His way" was a constant thread throughout the pages of her journals and published writings.

The thrill that I experienced in the first reading of this Lilias quotation came back in stronger power as I was preparing to write her biography. Could it be that I was part of that bigger plan to introduce, a century later, her timeless perspective to a time-driven generation? "*Stored-up sunrays waiting undimmed … only waiting to be given out.*"

> *Time is nothing to God: nothing in its speeding; nothing in its halting. He is the God that "inhabiteth eternity."*
>
> —*December 12, 1920*

Lord, I am so earthbound, so consumed in the here and now. Free me from the pursuit of results to the higher calling of faithfulness.

# THE PAIN OF PARTING

Great is thy faithfulness. The LORD is my portion, saith my soul; therefore will I hope in him. The LORD is good unto them that wait for him, to the soul that seeketh him.

LAMENTATIONS 3:23–25 KJV

*There is a wonderful sense of expansion—endless expansion—
about our love for those who are gone, as if it had escaped earthly fettering.
The pain of the parting is just the rending of the sheath, as it were,
to let the flower have its way. And their love for us will have grown
in the same way, only in fuller measure, into something pure
and fathomless and boundless and inexhaustible
because it is "in God."*

DIARY MAY 26, 1918

ONE YEAR AGO THIS WEEK, my mother went to the "Home" for which she longed. This first anniversary of her death brings to the surface vivid memories of the last months of her ninety-eight years.

Telephone calls had become almost a daily ritual. Often my creativity was challenged by "topics to talk about" as her world became increasingly limited (along with her hearing). There was something that would inevitably resonate: a shared memory … a Scripture verse … favorite songs sung, in duet, over the miles … events in her life (a health flare-up, a visit or letter, flowers outside her window, sometimes a tidbit of breaking news) … events in the lives of her grandchildren and great-grands, as she loved to call them.

Often our conversation would end with a prayer. "What would you like me to pray for you?" I would ask this person who had faithfully prayed for me (and mine) through the decades of my life. I would brace myself for what was becoming her stock answer: "Pray that God would take me Home." Stab to heart. I'd try to affirm her value. Now. Her prayers, her listening heart, her simply "being there" for her family, for *me* in recent transitions, her continuing to pioneer each life stage, modeling now what it looks like to "grow old gracefully." When my attempts seemed less than convincing, I would tease, "Well, I guess God just isn't ready for you quite yet." Invariably that would bring a rueful chuckle, "I guess not."

And so it was, one evening, the same routine, but this time with a surprise twist. To my "what do you want me to pray for you?" she paused, drew a deep breath, and answered, "Pray for me to have courage." Was it a health crisis she feared? Death? "Courage for what?" I asked. "Courage for *living*."

Courage for living. Is that not really the challenge we all face to one degree or another and in various forms? Joan Chittister observed in *Illuminated Life*, "One of the most difficult, but most seasoning elements of life is simply the fine art of getting up every morning, of doing what must be done if for no other reason than that it is our responsibility to do it. To face the elements of the day and keep on going takes a peculiar kind of courage. It is in dailiness that we prove our mettle. And it is not easy."

There are so many escape routes from, well, life. As a culture we have become escape artists from reality, numbing our feelings in substances or activities or people or things. We look for ways to avoid the source of our fears by skirting around the issues at hand or denying their very existence.

Often it is only when we have no other option that we are forced to look at our circumstances and ourselves confronting, at last, what it is that we fear.

My brother identifies "Life's Two Greatest Fears"—dying and living—in a sermon by the same name. I am grateful that we have had the privilege of having a mother who lived long enough to show her adult children both how to live and how to die. With *courage.* Whether it was in the big trials and tests of life or merely the tedium of seemingly endless days. Courage.

At the end of the day—literally our days on earth—comes "*a wonderful sense of expansion*"—the *"endless expansion"* of eternity with God. "He will wipe every tear from their eyes. There will be no more death or mourning or crying or pain" (Revelation 21:4). Yes, Mother has escaped earthly fettering, at last. And "*the pain of the parting is just the rending of the sheath, as it were, to let the flower have its way*"—to let her Savior have His sway.

Thank You, God, for providing for me a model of courage. Strengthen me to face my fears of living and help me to view the challenges of earth in the light of eternity.

IMAGES OF Spiritual Growth

AUGUST ORANGES

He has made everything beautiful in its time.
ECCLESIASTES 3:11

*All little miniature beginnings but all "beautiful in their time,"
like the dark green August oranges in the court below. The fact that they have got thus
far into being is more than a promise. Like all the promises of God they are
(given the conditions) an accomplishment begun.
"His 'Yea' only waits our 'Amen.'"*

DIARY AUGUST 11, 1906

I GAZE AT THE PICTURE posted on our daughter's Facebook wall. Three tow-haired children, toasted brown by the summer sun, freshly scrubbed, hair brushed and clad in brand new clothes—ready for their first day of school. They are sitting at the kitchen table, name holders identifying their place by their new classes: 6th Grader; 4th Grader; 1st Grader. Such an attitude of expectancy. Fresh start. New beginning.

There is something about new beginnings! Evelyn Bence captures the spirit of expectancy in the prologue of her compilation *New Beginnings: Celebrate the Fresh Starts of Life*:

> *A new beginning. A fresh start. A clean slate. There is something almost irresistible about a new beginning. Whether it's starting a new job, moving into a new home, enrolling in a new school, or beginning a new relationship, a new venture makes you feel like a child on the first day of school. Armed with a fistful of newly sharpened pencils and an unsoiled notebook tucked under your arm, you stand prepared for the new adventure. Your stomach flutters with anticipation as you face new challenges and new lessons. Lessons of courage and valor, perhaps. Certainly lessons of achievement and failure. But above all else, a new beginning represents hope.*

Hope! There is something about new beginnings that appeals to a universal (if latent) sense of hope. It holds the promise of something more—or different. A new chance. Change. Look at newness in nature: a seed, a bud, a sapling. Consider the same in humankind: a dream, a project, a job, a location. Perhaps we see it most in a newborn baby, untouched by life yet brimming with possibilities.

I remember holding our third (and last) newborn in my arms, listening to the song "I Am a Promise" on a Gaither Trio record (yes, record!) given to me by my mother. Perhaps it was the season (Christmas) or maybe hormones, but I was overcome with emotion as I considered the unknown possibilities in this little bundle of humanity: "You are a promise to be anything God wants you to be."

New beginnings signal all the above: possibility … promise … potentiality. This was the sermon the *dark green August oranges* preached to Lilias toward the end of what was arguably the three most difficult years in Algiers. The local government continually sabotaged their ministry through varied and creative forms of oppression, severely limiting their programs and reducing the involvement of the Arab people. Lilias's compromised health forced an extended period of rest away from the rigors of Algiers and, even upon return, months of continuing weakness limited her activities. There were disappointments with the closest of their Arab friends.

Yet even in the darkest months of unrelenting difficulty, inward and outward, there were rays of hope: *dark green August oranges* holding more than a promise in their new beginnings. First, there was an advance in literature: developing story parables firmly set in the context and customs of Algeria as well as a revision of parts of the New Testament into a truly colloquial Arabic.

Then, even more amazingly, came the opportunity to buy an old native house, in the nearby suburb of El Biar, at a sum only slightly greater than the less adequate cottage they sought for relief from the summer heat and humidity. Lilias viewed the rambling house crowning the hillside of vineyards and firwood and reveled in the possibilities for the future: a training center, a halfway house for fledgling believers, rallies for Christian workers, guest rooms for weary workers. "*It seemed like a fairy tale of dreams suddenly dropped down to earth—yet with a curious sense that it was no dream but a wonderful bit of God's unfoldings … Such visions come of what God might make of it & the only answer I get when I ask Him what it means is 'He Himself knew what He would do.'*"

"*Dark green August oranges*"—time alone would fully reveal God's plan but "*the fact that they got thus far into being is more than a promise of what was to come.*" Each individual "orange" indicated the promise of work begun and, "*like all the promises of God they are (given the conditions) an accomplishment begun.*"

Life is growth and change. It is never static. God has purposes and promises for what He intends for our lives. If only we listen. And are patient. We must faithfully tend the "dark green oranges"—not disparaging their size and color—as they are more than a promise of an accomplishment begun.

The key, I believe, is in the rest of the simple song, which encourages us to "listen to God's voice" with the assurance that we will "hear God's voice" and that He will help us to "make the right choice." The underlying message: with God's help we "can be anything God wants us to be." And, I would add, *do* anything He wants us to do. When we are attuned to God's voice, present to His Spirit then, as Lilias writes, "*His 'Yea' only waits our 'Amen.'*"

What are the *dark green August oranges* in my life? In your life? The beginning of a relationship … a new job … a move to a new location … the start (or restart) of a project or ministry … perhaps it is a new approach to an old situation or relationship … the embrace of a dream deferred.

> *"All little miniature beginnings are 'beautiful in their time,' like the dark green August oranges ... Like all the promises of God they are (given the conditions) an accomplishment begun."*

Lord, how I love fresh starts and new beginnings! May I tend faithfully the "small green oranges" in my life and trust You for the fulfillment of their inherent promise.

# GROWING POINTS

Forget the former things;
do not dwell on the past.
See, I am doing a new thing!
Now it springs up; do you not perceive it?
I am making a way in the wilderness
and streams in the wasteland.

ISAIAH 43:18-19

Growing points were the things that spoke to me on the journey through Italy. You can see them already on the bare boughs, waiting for the spring, and all the year through they are the most precious thing the plant has got, be it great or small, and the most shielded therefore from chance of harm. And the growing point of our soul is the thing with which the Spirit of God is specially dealing, and all depends on faithfulness there.

DIARY DECEMBER 23, 1900

ONE OF THE GREAT AND unexpected joys of retirement has been gardening—Dave tending; I cutting!—spurred, no doubt, by having been gifted a rose garden. Eight rose plants bring delight whether viewed outside or framed by the dining room window. Foliage or bloom, each aspect provides recreation: tilling the soil, tending the plants, watching buds unfurl to flower, choosing the perfect moment to cut and capture the blossom for display in silver bud vase or flask of cranberry glass.

Perhaps one of the prime pleasures, for Gardener Dave, is the daily examination of each individual bush for signs of new life: flush of red foliage signaling the advent of new buds. Daily, in season (almost year-round in Florida) he proudly proclaims the promise encapsulated in sheaths of green: ten buds … twenty-two buds … sixty-three buds! Each bud signals new life. Growing points. Each new growing point, whether a rose or any other plant, signals the same: hope, potential, promise. *Life*.

And as it is with the plant, so it is with the soul. Each new growing point indicates life. Many years ago I read a book by Bruce Larson, *Living on the Growing Edge*. The title has challenged me to this day. Larson observed a remarkable teacher known not only for her effective teaching of young students, but for her ability to help them understand themselves and life. He asked her about her method. She explained that she tried to be aware of the "growing edge" of each student. The growing edge, it seems, is that area where the student is ready and able to learn. A good teacher must know what a student needs to learn and is ready to learn, and then present the student with that material.

Larson makes his point:

> *Surely this is how the Holy Spirit wants to work in each of our lives. Every one of us has a spiritual growing edge. We all have mastered certain skills and subjects and disciplines and formed certain attitudes. Our tendency is to sit back and make this the sum and substance of the Christian experience. On the other hand God says, "Well done," and then moves us on to new areas that we can grasp and master.*

It is, in reality, much easier to stay put, so to speak, to play to the middle ground of one's particular area of strength. Maybe, even a bit smugly, measure others by that strength and come out winning. But growth, real growth, is pushing out to the edge of our experience—to our personal growing edge—out of our safety zone into new life. In the realm of art, it has been said that an artist never stands still. One is either growing or dying. The same could be said in the life of the soul. Faith that huddles in the security of the known is a faith that repeats itself, without moving out to the edge, toward God's even greater intentions for us.

 Countless examples in every disciple illustrate this concept. But here I think of my mother in the final decade of her life. Old-school, by generation and temperament, she gloried in her role as "support partner" to her husband. We as a family watched her redefine her role, to accommodate her husband's failing health, taking the lead for herself and her mate. Then as a widow she restructured her world, to better connect with her geographically scattered family. She remembered the names of her sixteen great-grandchildren by group photos from which she prayed for them. At age ninety-two she started writing her memoirs, to impart her legacy of faith to her family. While I knew that she kept up with world and national events, it wasn't until her memorial service that I learned the scope of her reading. She read the sports pages of the *Chicago Tribune,* just to keep informed and conversant with her grandson-in-law's interest in the Pittsburgh Steelers. She passed along her copy of *Psychology for Living* to another grandson-in-law who was a clinical psychologist.

 "Living on the growing edge" will mean different things to different people. It will mean different things for the same person at various seasons of life. For my mother, an introvert by nature, it meant pushing herself in many directions to connect with her family and remain active in an increasingly foreign world. The growing point of a soul may be, like Mother's, determined by response to a radical life event … it might be opening oneself to a challenging experience or point of view; it could be developing a new skill to open new doors of opportunity, or swallowing one's pride by releasing one's "right to be right" for the restoration of a relationship. It might require embracing new ways of doing things in music or worship … taking a risk, even in the face of possible failure … being more active if we are reflective by bent or vice versa.

Living on the growing edge. Growing points. At the end of the day, it is not a senseless arbitrary action, jumping to the unknown or untried. Rather, it is being attentive to the working of God's Spirit in our souls. *"The growing edge of our soul is the thing with which the Spirit of God is specially dealing and all depends on faithfulness there."*

Lord, reveal to me the growing points of my soul. Help me not to be stuck in the security of the past but to be open to change and growth.

HOW SILENTLY, SO SILENTLY

*But grow in the grace and knowledge of our L*ORD *and Savior Jesus Christ.*

2 PETER 3:18

All that outworking of His Grace has come so silently—"not with observation"—like His work in all growth around—so that one can hardly tell when or how the expansion has come.

DIARY MARCH 9, 1923

PAINTING FROM JOURNAL 1893

"*ALL THAT OUTWORKING OF HIS Grace has come so silently.*" Lilias reflects, as was her practice, on the anniversary of their first setting foot on North African terrain: March 9, 1888. This year, however, was their thirty-fifth anniversary, more than sufficient time to look back and observe significant evidence of "expansion" in their ministry.

She reflects on the very nature of growth, noting that this is like God's work in all growth. Whether physical or spiritual, we just don't see or hear growth happen!

This is, perhaps, most obvious in the physical world. Periodic visits with our young grandchildren, even after only a few months' absence, invariably elicit the "my, how you've grown" response (no matter how we try to check that overworked welcome). A chart documenting their growth, age, and date verifies the same. But no one—present parents, absent grandparents—ever observed the very moments of growth. *Silently* … without observation.

Look at nature. Take a flower or a tree, for instance. Rarely (if ever) do we see or hear a flower open or a tree leaf out. But they do. *Silently* … without observation … season after season, year after year.

This past week was a return in time, in which this principle of growth was vividly witnessed. We attended a high school reunion, meeting schoolmates, some of whom we had not seen for half a century. (Name tags do help!) A reunion dinner concluded with reminiscences and current updates. Time had transformed untested teens—awkward, silly, wild, crazy, shy, earnest, driven—into full-blown adults, who have evolved, for the most part, into persons of depth, caring, and maturity. Growth: *silently* ... without observation.

On an even more personal note, we took a sentimental journey back to the house of my youth, now boasting a stately pin oak tree, straight as an arrow, piercing the sky, great leafy branches shading much of the front lawn. This tree was the subject of much merriment when first planted. Based on careful research, my mother planted it with high hopes for its potential beauty and shade. Virtually a stick in the ground, it barely made it through the first season. Second season, she braced it with a pyramid of wire cords to correct a very definite bend. How we loved to tease Mother as we witnessed the seasons of struggle. But she held fast to her hopes. Now, decades later, we stopped the car, allowing me to pick up a fallen leaf to press in my journal. A reminder of the character of growth: *silently* ... without observation.

The process of growth, by its very character, whether physical or spiritual, is contrary to what we by nature desire. We want results. Now. We want evidence that our efforts count. Society rewards and, for that matter, punishes by the same mentality. A losing season can cost a coach his job. An employee may be demoted or dismissed by failure to demonstrate results. The same mentality invades the ecclesiastical world: the number of people or programs—observable results (!)—becomes the measure of success.

So it is with our souls. We want results. Now. We resolve to do what it takes to become people of maturity. We read a chapter of Scripture, go to a Bible study or retreat, attend church, tackle a service project. It is so hard to measure the growth of a soul, but this we know: we often fall short of being the people we yearn to be.

Lilias concludes her reflections with a helpful insight on growth: "*All one can tell is that we have had nothing to do with its evolution except a measure of blind obedience—& oh that that measure had been fuller.*" Just as there are certain conditions that assure growth in the physical world—fertile soil, moisture, sun—there are conditions for growth in the world of the spirit. Our souls must be fed, yes, and we must be obedient to God's voice as we live out our lives of faith. For the most part it simply involves faithfulness to what we know we should do: asking, listening, obeying.

The transformation of the human heart, like all growth, is slow. It is a process by which, through time and intent, we develop the habit of divine orientation. We can no more identify each moment of our spirit's growth than we can the progress of a child to adult or a sapling to majestic tree. And yet, silently, without observation, our hearts are taking on a new character as we move quietly closer to God.

How silently, how silently, the wondrous gift is given!
So God imparts to human hearts the blessings of His heaven.

PHILLIPS BROOKS

Lord, reveal to me the growing points of my soul. Help me not to be stuck in the security of the past but to be open to change and growth.

THE ROOTS OF SPIRITUAL CREATION

For with you is the fountain of life.

PSALM 36:9

Today's find was beautiful to the inward vision as well as to the outward. It was clusters of exquisite wild lilies—white and fragile and fragrant—growing out of the hot salt sand that drifts into dunes round the stunted juniper and lentisk bushes that fringe the shore. Down below the surface, the storage of reserve material in the lily bulbs had silently taken place ... and there they had lain, shrouded and waiting. The hour had come now, and no adverse condition could keep back the upspringing. The same Lord over all can store the roots in His spiritual creation, even though they have but smothering sand drifts around them.

JULY 22, 1909; SAND LILIES

THE IMAGE OF SAND LILIES was one that touched the heart of Lilias not only aesthetically but spiritually. She marveled at the pristine blossom, "*white and fragile and fragrant,*" that managed somehow not only to survive the hostile desert but, in fact, to flourish: "*laughing to scorn the difficulties of their environment.*" Nourished by a hidden source of energy, "*their life was stored away, out of sight and there was enough for all the need.*"

She drew hope from this visual parable, hope that the spiritual dormancy she witnessed in a barren land would result, in God's timing, in a "*sudden miracle bloom out of these parched countries, and to show that He is 'King over all the earth.'*" The painting of sand lilies featured above was reproduced from the cover of a little booklet presenting both her belief in a day of dawning spiritually and a plea for prayers on behalf of that vision. Frequently the image of the "sand lily" would appear in her various writings circulated among fellow missionaries and partners in prayer.

The sand lily has taken on another meaning for me, first, in relation to Lilias who aptly was called Lily by her friends. Studying archives of her childhood, I witnessed the English Lily, nurtured in an ideal garden climate—rich, well-drained soil, moist air, sheltered site—the perfect environment for a pristine lily. All the natural resources—heredity, home environment, intellectual and artistic stimulation, spiritual nurture—would become "stored energy," spiritually speaking, requisite for survival in the harsh Algerian soil. The *Desert* Lily!

Then I consider the implications of this concept of "stored spiritual energy" for myself, for others. Scripture, on the one hand, speaks of a kind of "spiritual currency" that, in God's economy, is not stored in advance to draw upon at will but given directly by God, to meet the need of a given situation. On the other hand, not contradictory to that special dispensation of "grace," is the continual challenge of Scripture to be "rooted and built up" in Christ, "strengthened in the faith as you were taught" (Colossians 2:7). As with Lilias, certain factors contribute to the formation of our souls: heredity, environment, nurture, experiences good and difficult. Scripture continually challenges us to turn over all things—good and bad; past and present—to God for Him to work for our good … for the growth of our souls.

There is a strong parallel to physical training and spiritual formation. Just as a person builds strength and endurance through certain physical disciplines, we build a muscular faith by *spiritual* disciplines that sustain us daily and provide inner support in times of duress: meditation on Scripture, prayer, worship, service, fellowship with other believers. One could say that we are cultivating "stored energy" to be drawn upon in time of drought, when our soil is parched, no rain in sight. Desert lilies.

God has promised to be a "spring of living water" (Jeremiah 17:13). In turn, we "will be like a tree (lily!) planted by the water that sends out its roots by the stream." You or I can be the one who "has no worries in a year of drought and never fails to bear fruit" (Jeremiah 17:8).

God, You are the spring of living water. May I intentionally drink from that water and be nourished by Your Word.

SOUL FOOD

Thy words were found, and I did eat them; and thy word was unto me the joy and rejoicing of mine heart: for I am called by thy name, O Lord God of hosts.

JEREMIAH 15:16 KJV

When Moses went in before the Lord to speak with Him, he took the veil off.
Bare absolute contact with God's Presence—if our times alone with Him were
but that all the time, they would be mighty in their outcome.

DIARY AUGUST 16, 1901

PAINTING FROM POCKET SKETCHBOOK, FRANCE/SWITZERLAND/VENICE, 1877

I LINGERED IN FRONT OF the dessert table, studying the slices of cake arranged on white plastic plates. I became aware that I was blocking a man behind me and sheepishly admitted, "I was looking for the one with the most frosting." He responded, "Take your time. I'm looking for the one with the *least* frosting." Noting his trim physique, I ruefully acknowledged, "This, in microcosm, explains a significant difference between the two of us."

Amy Carmichael, in her daily devotional *Whispers of His Power,* quotes an old English nursery rhyme:

> *It's a very odd thing,*
> *As odd as can be,*
> *That whatever she eats*
> *Turns into Miss T.*

She elaborates: "If we hastily read God's word, without taking the time to absorb it, we do not gain much. But if we take it *into* ourselves (Thy word was found and I did eat it), then it becomes part of us. It 'turns into Miss T.'"

"You are what you eat." How many times have we heard that principle in relation to our physical well-being? It is just as applicable to the spiritual realm. We are profoundly affected by what we feed our souls. What better place to develop a basic, healthy menu than with a steady diet of Scripture: God's revealed Word. *Soul* food.

Lilias was keenly aware of needing "soul food" if she was to survive the challenges of her pioneer work in Algeria. Her yearly pattern allowed for a European break, including a fortnight "alone with God," frequently scheduled around family or ministry commitments. The exact site was often a matter of prayer and the *"little traces by which God leads us in the way of His steps,"* a story in itself.

Such was the case in September 1901, when she settled in an alpine village above Zermatt, in Switzerland. *"Up again tonight in a beloved Findelu—alone this time, & for a fortnight—such a gift from God for time with Him. It is looking lovelier than ever with the first tawny touches of autumn on the bilberry bushes."* The driving force for her annual (and daily) retreats was one and the same: a soul hunger for God almost visceral in its intensity.

I searched her diaries and journals to discern a formula for her "times alone with God"—a Bible reading program, perhaps, or certain disciplines that would instruct my spiritual formation.

To no avail. But I did discover some common elements to her "diet." For starters, I noted a ravishing hunger for God that led her to seek out places conducive to communion with Him, whether it be a quiet spot in a nearby woods or palm garden, a "place of prayer" in a rooftop room or desert outpost. There she drew a circle of quiet around her "bare soul" and waited for God to speak, through His world, His Word, and through a collection of topically related Scriptures compiled in her well-worn leather volume, *Daily Light*. More often than not, God spoke first through His created order—daisy, dandelion, snow-diamond, firwood—which, in turn, connected her to Scripture: The peak of the Matterhorn "*linked on with that verse in Job.*" And, "*The thistles here are a commentary to me on that wonderful title of 1 Timothy 1:11, 'The Blissful God.'*" And the fog "*has been linking in, these days, with the 'forty days with God, of the Bible.'*" From there the conversation continues, she "*tracing in Scripture*" these lessons and/or thoughts; she bringing them back to God for His instruction.

 I am very much a novice when it comes to that kind of communion with God. But I believe it possible. And I do desire it. Prosaic soul that I am, I can't depend on my "beholdings" to lead me to the heights and depths of Lilias's experience; I have found value in a daily Bible reading schedule, particularly the Scripture Union Bible Reading Program, *Encounter with God*. It provides a plan that leads me in a systematic way through the Bible (Old Testament once and the New Testament twice every five years) guided by a brief commentary on each passage, written by a variety of trusted biblical scholars. Whitney Kuniholm, president of Scripture Union/USA warns in a "Final Note" at the end of the current guide: "We must always remember that the point of the method is to meet God, to become more aware of him, to be in step with his Spirit. We learn the discipline because it puts us in a position to experience God."

Eugene Peterson sums this thought: "'Eat this book' is my metaphor of choice for focusing attention on what is involved in reading our Holy Scriptures formatively, that is, in a way that the Holy Spirit uses them to form Christ in us. We are not interested in knowing more but in becoming more … This kind of reading … enters our souls as food, enters our stomachs, spreads through our blood, and becomes holiness and love and wisdom."

Lord, increase my appetite for You. May I hunger for the soul food that results in a healthy, resilient spiritual life.

EXPECT GOD TO TRIUMPH

No discipline seems pleasant at the time, but painful. Later on, however, it produces a harvest of righteousness and peace for those who have been trained by it.

HEBREWS 12:11

Take the very hardest thing in your life—the place of difficulty, outward or inward, and expect God to triumph gloriously in that very spot. Just there He can bring your soul into blossom.

PARABLES OF THE CROSS

THIS IS ONE OF MY favorite Lilias quotes. It rings with victorious affirmation. It speaks to the deepest pain. I'm tempted to quote it verbatim and leave it alone. I can't improve on the wording or, for that matter, on the content. While it can rightly stand on its own, it does bear examination. What, really, does it mean? More to the point, is it true? Does it have any practical bearing in my life today?

"*Take the hardest thing in your life … and expect God to triumph gloriously in that very spot.*" We all know stories of hardship and difficulty and how people have triumphed in spite of, or perhaps because of, that very difficulty. The periodic Olympic events provide countless testimonials, showing a crowning achievement as the proportional result of hardship endured, difficulty overcome. No pain, no gain is also borne out in the spiritual realm. Difficulty endured produces something yet stronger. The greater the difficulty, the greater the triumph.

But there is a unique aspect to her claim that goes beyond the formulaic gain for pain. It is the promise of a triumph that transcends *our* efforts and resources to a work of *God* in the very place of our potential defeat. "*Expect God to triumph gloriously in that very spot.*" Not only will God bring triumph in the place of pain, but He will go beyond the particular need of the moment to the transformation of one's very soul: "*Just there He can bring your soul into blossom!*"

In her devotional classic *Parables of the Cross*, Lilias illuminates this truth with a parallel from nature. In delicate watercolors she paints a bit of gorse bush, branches bristling with thorns, large and small, stuck out in all directions. The thorns have been hardening and sharpening throughout the year, and even with the arrival of spring they do not drop off or soften. But halfway up the pictured thorn appears two brown furry balls, mere specks at first, that break at last, straight out of last year's thorn, into a blaze of golden glory!

Our hardest difficulties, outward and inward, are like those thorns, uncompromising and seemingly without relief. There is no apparent solution. No way out. No end in sight. They bring us to the point of deepest despair. We are dogged with questions: Where do we turn? How do we proceed? Sometimes there seems to be no good reason to keep going on.

It is here that the God of the gorse thorns looks down on us with love and says, "Do not despair. Nothing can happen to you that I cannot manage. Trust me." Elisabeth Elliot in *A Path through Suffering,* her reflection on this parable, writes,

> *He wants to transform every form of human suffering into something glorious. He can redeem it. He can bring life out of death. Every event of our lives provides*

> *opportunity to learn the deepest lesson anyone can learn on earth ... When our souls lie barren in a winter which seems hopeless and endless, God has not abandoned us. His work goes on. He asks our acceptance of the painful process and our trust that He will indeed give resurrection life.*

I can look back over my life and see where pain was requisite for God's transforming work. I see evidence of this principle in the great heroes of the faith, biblical and more recent history. Then there are stories related to me that will never make the pages of history. But what about the here and now? Can I—can *we*—take the thorns that seem so unrelentingly hard and expect God to triumph in that very place? Fears for a loved one or for our own future ... pain or disability that makes life unbearable ... betrayal of a supposed friend or family member ... injustice or misunderstanding in the workplace or no job at all ... presence of a demanding person in our household ... financial insecurity and limited resources ... Can we believe that out of that very thorn will come a blossom fragrant and glorious? Can we trust that out of that difficulty God will bring our soul into blossom?

This quote, illuminated by the simple gorse bush, presents the *problem*—difficulty, outward and inward; the *process*—take it to God with the expectation that *He* will triumph in that very place; and the *product*—a soul brought into glorious blossom!

Blest be the Architect, whose art
Could build so strong in a weak heart.

GEORGE HERBERT

God, I bring to You the trials and tribulations of my life, trusting You to bring my "soul into blossom" at those very points of difficulty.

RELATED RESOURCES

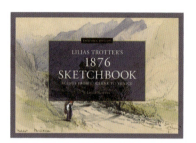

FACSIMILE EDITION

Lilias Trotter's 1876 Sketchbook: Scenes from Lucerne to Venice

ORIGINAL UNPUBLISHED ARTWORK BY LILIAS TROTTER

AVAILABLE ON AMAZON

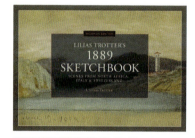

FACSIMILE EDITION

Lilias Trotter's 1889 Pocket Sketchbook: Scenes of North Africa, Italy and Switzerland

ORIGINAL UNPUBLISHED ARTWORK BY LILIAS TROTTER

AVAILABLE ON AMAZON

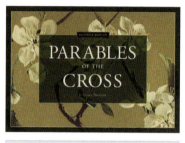

FACSIMILE EDITION

Parables of the Cross

BY I. LILIAS TROTTER

AVAILABLE ON AMAZON

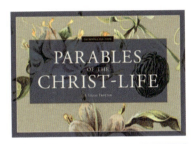

FACSIMILE EDITION

Parables of the Christ-life

BY I. LILIAS TROTTER

AVAILABLE ON AMAZON

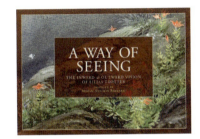

A Way of Seeing: The Inward and Outward Vision of Lilias Trotter

COMPILED BY
MIRIAM HUFFMAN ROCKNESS

AVAILABLE ON AMAZON

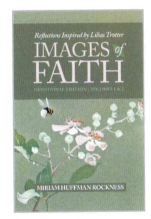

Images of Faith: Devotional Edition, Reflections Inspired by Lilias Trotter Vol. 1 & 2

MIRIAM HUFFMAN ROCKNESS

AVAILABLE ON AMAZON

MORE RELATED RESOURCES

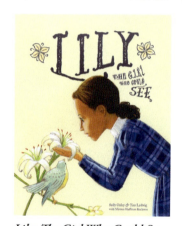

Lily: The Girl Who Could See

A CHILDREN'S BOOK BY SALLY OXLEY & TIM LADWIG WITH MIRIAM HUFFMAN ROCKNESS

AVAILABLE ON AMAZON

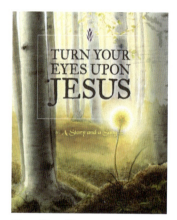

Turn Your Eyes upon Jesus: A Story and a Song

ILLUSTRATED GIFT BOOK FOR CHILDREN OR ADULTS BY MIRIAM HUFFMAN ROCKNESS WITH ILLUSTRATIONS BY TIM LADWIG

AVAILABLE ON AMAZON

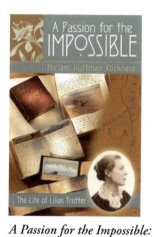

A Passion for the Impossible: The Life of Lilias Trotter

BY MIRIAM HUFFMAN ROCKNESS

Published by Discovery House Publishers

A Blossom in the Desert
BY MIRIAM HUFFMAN ROCKNESS
Published by Discovery House Publishers

MANY BEAUTIFUL THINGS

THE LIFE AND VISION OF LILIAS TROTTER

WATCH THE FEATURE-LENGTH DOCUMENTARY EXPLORING THE LIFE OF LILIAS TROTTER

Watch the trailer

liliastrotter.com/many-beautiful-things

Explore & learn about Lilias Trotter

liliastrotter.com

A documentary by award-winning filmmaker
LAURA WATERS HINSON
Featuring **MICHELLE DOCKERY** of **DOWNTON ABBEY**
as the voice of **LILIAS TROTTER**

If you enjoyed the book, please consider leaving a review where you purchased it, or on Goodreads to **help us encourage other readers to discover the rich legacy of Lilias Trotter**. You can also follow us on Facebook, Instagram, and Twitter. Thank you.

SAY HELLO!

WEBSITES	liliastrotter.com
FACEBOOK	facebook.com/liliastrotterlegacy
INSTAGRAM	@liliastrotterlegacy
TWITTER	@lilias_trotter
EMAIL	info@liliastrotter.com

Printed in Poland
by Amazon Fulfillment
Poland Sp. z o.o., Wrocław